3rd MILLENNIUM

THE CHALLENGE AND THE VISION

3rd Millennium

The Challenge and the Vision

The Club of Budapest
Report on Creative Paths of
Human Evolution

Ervin Laszlo
Foreword by
Sir Peter Ustinov

A GAIA CLASSIC
Gaia Books Limited

A GAIA CLASSIC
Books from Gaia celebrate the vision of Gaia, and seek to help readers live in greater personal and planetary harmony.

Editor	Charlie Ryrie
Managing Editor	Pip Morgan
Production	Lyn Kirby
Direction and Design	Patrick Nugent

First published in the United Kingdom in 1997 by
Gaia Books Ltd, 66 Charlotte St, London W1P 1LR
and 20 High St, Stroud, Glos GL5 1AS

ISBN 1 85675 068 X

A catalogue record of this book is available from the British Library.

10 9 8 7 6 5 4 3 2 1

Ervin Laszlo:

President of the Club of Budapest, Ervin Laszlo is one of the foremost thinkers and scientists of our age. Among his many responsibilities, he is currently the Science Director of the International University of Peace in Berlin; Founder and Director of the General Evolution Research Group; Administrateur of the Université Interdisciplinaire de Paris (UIP); Advisor to the Director-General of UNESCO, and to the International Yehudi Menuhin Foundation; Fellow of the World Academy of Arts and Science; Member of the International Academy of Sciences, the Senate of the International Medici Academy, and the International Academy of Philosophy of Science, and Associate Member of the Club of Rome. He has also held positions as the Professor of Philosophy at the State University of New York; visiting Professor of Music and Aesthetics at Indiana University; visiting Professor of Philosophy at Northwestern University; visiting Professor of Futures Studies at the University of Houston; visiting Professor of Systems Science at Portland State University, and visiting Professor of Peace Studies at Kyung Hee University. He is a fellow of Yale, Princeton and Gothenburg Universities, and founded the Vienna Academy for the Study of the Future and the European Academy of Evolutionary Studies. He was Programme Director for the United Nations Institute for Training and Research (UNITAR), and General Secretary of the European Culture Impact Research Consortium (EUROCIRCON).

Ervin Laszlo has written 66 books, which have been translated into 17 languages, edited a four volume Encyclopedia and produced several hundred papers and articles. He has also recorded seven long playing records of classical piano music. A list of his recent publications can be found on page 148.

CONTENTS

THE CLUB OF BUDAPEST is an informal association of leading artists, scientists, writers, spiritual persons and creative individuals from all spheres, who have come together in recognition of the urgent need to evolve a new consciousness. The philosophy, aims and activities of the Club are described on pages 127-143 of this book.

Honorary Members of the Club of Budapest:

CHINGIZ AITMATOV

A.T. ARIYARATNE

MAURICE BÉJART

THOMAS BERRY

ARTHUR C. CLARKE

XIV DALAI LAMA

RIANE EISLER

MILOS FORMAN

ALUKA GOLANI

ARPÁD GÖNCZ

MIKHAIL GORBHACHEV

OTTO HEBERT HAJEK

PIR VILYAT INAYAT KHAN

MIKLÓS JANCSÓ

KEN-ICHIRO KOBAYASHI

GIDON KREMER

ÉVA MARTON

ZUBIN MEHTA

LORD YEHUDI MENUHIN

EDGAR MITCHELL

EDGAR MORIN

ROBERT MULLER

UTE-HENRIETTE OHOVEN

GILLO PONTECORVO

RÚHÍYYIH RABBANI

JEAN-PIERRE RAMPAL

JOSEF ROTBLAT

PETER RUSSELL

KARAN SINGH

LIV ULLMANN

SIR PETER USTINOV

VIGDÍS FINNBOGADÓTTIR

RICHARD VON WEIZSÄCKER

ELIE WEISEL

BETTY WILLIAMS

MOHAMMED YUNUS

Recently deceased Members:

WILLIS HARMAN

SIR GEORG SOLTI

FOREWORD

by Sir Peter Ustinov

The Club of Budapest is not so much a reunion of kindred spirits as a collection of people who realize that the problems of tomorrow cannot be met by the logic of today; even less so by the norms of the past. Ervin Laszlo is the original visionary of the organization, it is he who has inspired those of necessarily different backgrounds and temperaments to join him in this great adventure of stretching human imagination beyond its normal limits to encounter the challenges of a rapidly changing society on equal terms.

His first question, and one to all hopeful explorers, is "Where are we going?" It is necessary to assess this if we wish to know where not to go. The path resounds to our footfall, but do we have it in ourselves to change direction?

Of course, we cannot but be optimistic. And basically, this is a book about optimism. Pessimists have no need to stretch the mind. The role for the individual is to think globally, thereby living responsibly. This entails the creation of a new enterprise culture, and lifting the sights of governments, perhaps the most onerous task of all, as we glimpse beyond the myth of the Nation State. Ervin Laszlo affirms the need for a code for environmental morality, and a consequent culture of interexistence. And even, ideally, of interexistence, finding unity in the very diversity which seems to separate us, but only as holders of prescribed passports, not as members of the human race.

Ervin Laszlo enumerates the creative paths of human evolution, passing by way of Science, inevitably also by Art and Religion, which could be categorized as Culture, and by what he calls Alternative and Youth culture. He concludes by looking at what remains to be done – until the next reassessment that is, for the thinking must be open-ended, if its rules are not to be petrified with the passage of never-ending time.

This book is a challenge to the original thinker, to the pioneer, to the creative genius of mankind. Ervin Laszlo, the eminent scientist, lays before us some unexpected weapons in our armoury. The concept of matter, the nature of life, and last but not least, the power of the mind.

I leave you in all confidence to provide your own variations on the themes he has so meticulously and majestically laid before us.

PETER USTINOV
September 1997

PREFACE

We live in the midst of the fastest and most profound transformation in the history of humanity. This current transformation may be more profound than that which led from the Middle Ages to the modern industrial age, and it is occurring in a matter of decades rather than centuries. As the third millennium dawns on us, we find ourselves in a world where more people have more needs and make more demands than ever before, yet where human life and activity are penetrated and molded by globally circulating information, global environmental impacts, global markets, globe-spanning technologies, and globally effective political, managerial, professional, and lifestyle decisions. The conditions created by increased information and the globalization of life and society make the opening decades of the third millennium at least as different from the Modern Age as that age was different from the Middle Ages.

Living and acting in the new conditions calls for radically different ways of thinking and acting. This poses a problem, because the speed with which the post-modern age is breaking on us has not given us time to evolve the required insights and practices. For the most part, our generation attempts to cope with the conditions of the coming 21st century with the thinking and practices of the 20th. This, however, is like attempting to live in today's industrial societies with the mind-set of medieval villages. It is ineffective and, because of the vulnerability of current social and ecological structures, dangerous. The danger concerns every-one. Because of the increasing links and dependencies forged by global markets, technologies, and information, lagging perceptions and practices in one segment of society are a threat to all others.

The challenge of our time is to evolve the ways of living and acting that are suitable for the post-modern world into which we are projecting ourselves. Einstein told us that we cannot solve a problem with the same kind of thinking that gave rise to that problem. Translated to the end of the second millennium, this means that we cannot reach the beginning of the third without evolving the kind of thinking that would be appropriate to our changing conditions.

Evolving a new way of thinking calls for a great deal of creativity. To live in the third millennium we shall need more than incremental improvements on our current rationality; we shall need new thinking joined with new ways of perceiving and visioning ourselves, others, nature and the world around us. We shall need new values, ethics, and modes of life and behavior. Looking backwards will be of limited value: though history holds important lessons, it never fully repeats itself. Society, nature itself, evolves, changes, transforms. Though we are still members of a species that has existed genetically unchanged for the past hundred thousand years, our identity and roles have changed even in the course of the past decade. We must discover these anew in the context of the third millennium. In globe-spanning and interacting conditions, we must maintain our uniqueness, yet evolve a vision and a consciousness capable of embracing life on a small planet, swimming in the vast expanse of interstellar space.

In the 1970s, The Club of Rome made us aware of the limits to growth. In the 1980s, the ecological movement highlighted the importance of safeguarding our life-supporting environment. Now, at the end of this crucial century, The Club of Budapest calls attention to the need to evolve the consciousness — the vision, the ethics, and the modes of thinking, feeling and acting — required to live wisely and responsibly in the globally connected but individually, socially, and culturally diversified world of the third millennium.

PART ONE

WHERE ARE WE GOING?

At the turn of a century, people suspect that major changes are about to break on them. At the turn of the millennium this suspicion is still stronger: it gives rise to grand flights of fantasy. The optimistic variety of "millennium myths" speak of a new Golden Age, a New Jerusalem, the Peaceable Kingdom, the City of the Sun, or the Age of Aquarius. They foretell the arrival of the Messiah, Matriaya, Pahan, or Quetzalcoatl. The pessimistic variety predict a world devastated by comets, floods, or fire, a population decimated by starvation, disease and war, and even the coming of the Antichrist.

Level-headed people dismiss such fantasies: they know that just because there is a major change in the calendar there need not be a major change in the world. But is it true in today's world that we can exclude all varieties of change — even major change? The sense that the coming of the third millennium brings another world with it is curiously pronounced. Could it be a valid premonition of the shape of things to come? It would indeed be remarkable if the coming of the new millennium does coincide with the coming of a New Age, if such speculations turn out to be more than the figment of the imagination of sensitive but discontented young people, and cultivated but other-worldly intellectuals. The issue merits attention. Is there evidence for the possible coincidence of the dawn of the third millennium and the coming of a new world?

CHAPTER 1

THE PATH UNDER OUR FEET

Changes are in the air — wherever we look there are threats and problems. Economic growth, though it has been the major and most promising engine of development for the past two centuries, is creating mounting unemployment, widening income gaps, trade disputes, environmental degradation, and waves of migrants moving from the countryside to the urban centers, and from poor to richer countries. Nuclear power, though holding the promise of unlimited power supply, is conjuring up the specter of nuclear accidents, whether through technical breakdown or terrorist action, and posing as yet unsolved puzzles regarding the disposal of nuclear wastes and the decommissioning of aging reactors. Modern medicine, one of the proudest achievements of Western civilization, seems stymied in the face of the HIV epidemic and the recurrence of diseases such as bubonic plague in India, the ebola virus in Africa, and drug-resistant tuberculosis in America, while its applications create a plethora of new and increasingly antibiotics-resistant micro-organisms.

Information technology's cyberspace is connecting all parts of the world, and potentially all people, with two-way flows of communication and interaction, but it is also creating a new medium for crime, for intolerant cultural influences, pornography, and information warfare. Income gaps and uneven development are fueling more and more severe and frequent religious, ethnic, and racial conflicts. Organized crime is growing into a global enterprise with a gamut of activities ranging from information fraud to traffic in arms, drugs and human organs. Terrorism is graduating from conventional explosives to computer viruses, and to chemical, biological and nuclear weapons, and is also forming alliances with organized crime. And the population of this increasingly vulnerable and chaotic world keeps growing, to a projected 10 billion by the year 2030.

On first sight it seems difficult if not impossible to find one's way through today's maze of acute threats and latent possibilities. A clearer picture emerges, however, when we separate problems that can be handled with current methods and technologies, and those that require a deeper shift in attitudes and behaviors. The latter are likely to be more fundamental — they may underlie the conundrum of threats and problems that appear on the surface.

What, then, are the fundamental problems of our time? They can be grasped by referring to trends and processes, not static states and conditions. The trends and processes that generate the problems have existed for a long time, but now their unfolding is approaching a critical threshold. There are two problem-generating trends with overwhelming significance:

• the worldwide growth of the human family and its use of the planet's physical resources and biological life-support systems;

• the accelerating depletion of many of the planet's physical resources, and impairment of its biological life-support systems.

The size of the human population, multiplied by the amount of resources it uses and the waste and pollution it generates, specifies the load placed on the planet's physical resources and biological systems. But the physical resources are in finite supply, and the biological life-support systems are progressively impaired. Given the continuation of these trends, it is merely a matter of time before the two curves will intersect. At that point humanity's demands will exceed the planet's existing supplies and potentially regenerative capacities. We are already feeling the approach of this critical threshold — not only in the environmental domain, but also in the spheres of production, consumption, politics, personal lifestyles, employment, professional goals, and community life.

This is an unprecedented situation. Critical planetary thresholds were not reached at the dawn of the first millennium, nor at the dawn of the 20th century. But they are being rapidly approached at the turn of the third millennium. This should give us pause for some serious thinking — and unrelenting re-thinking.

The big picture

We must look first at the overall framework within which to place today's threats and problems. Humanity is part of the living web of life on this planet. It is part of nearly four billion years of biological evolution, and five million years of hominid evolution. Our own species, *Homo sapiens sapiens*, emerged about a hundred thousand years ago, but its numbers muliplied significantly only within living memory. The human population reached one billion — one thousand million — in the middle of the 19th century, and is growing toward six billion at the dawn of the 21st.

But numbers alone do not make for today's problems. Six billion humans still constitute only about 0.014 per cent of the biomass of life on Earth, and 0.44 per cent of the biomass of animals. Such a small fragment should not constitute a threat for the entire system, and hence for itself. Yet humanity does. Its impact is entirely out of proportion to its size. Humanity's impact on the biosphere is a growing load on, and progressive impairment of, the planet's life-support systems. This impact cannot increase indefinitely.

A finite system, with finite space, resources, and regenerative powers, has upper limits as to the load it can support. We may now be testing the effective range of these limits. This should not come as a surprise. Since the publication of *The Limits to Growth*, the first Report to The Club of Rome in 1972, the existence of "outer limits" to the carrying capacity of the planet has become common — though not necessarily welcome — knowledge. For the most part people have managed to convince themselves that such limits are theoretical, or that they are irrelevant, that there are either no absolute limits to human socioeconomic growth, or if there are, they are far enough in the future not to concern us. Such thinking allows people to believe that our generation, and even our children's generation, can live and grow within the outer limits of the planet, pushing them further back through more efficient technologies, and through the exploitation of new sources of energy and fresh reserves of raw materials. Therefore, at least for the foreseeable future, progress based on economic growth can continue unchanged.

This belief appeared justified in the 1970s, when two decades of steady growth seemed to have given sufficient proof of it. But it is mistaken just the same. By the year 2000 there will be over four billion people eager to live like they believe people do in the rich parts of America, Europe and Japan. If they do not succeed in moving toward this goal, poverty and frustration may erupt into breakdown and violence. And if that happens, the stable and linear growth trend, familiar from the recent past, will turn unstable and nonlinear. In complex energy- and resource-intensive systems, stresses and strains beyond the thresholds of dynamic stability lead to sudden changes — to what systems- and chaos-theorists describe as "bifurcations." We may now be approaching a series of sudden, system-level changes, an age of bifurcations.

It is in our own interest to deflect the further unfolding of the human load and planetary support capacity trends. Since we cannot halt population growth (though we can reduce its rate), the brunt of our attention must focus on safeguarding the integrity of the biological environment and diminishing the load placed on it (and on the stocks of needed physical resources), through unnecessary, wasteful, or harmful practices. We need to recognize that many of the physical resources we are using are nonrenewable, and that biological resources may be renewable but are used too rapidly for the stocks to be replenished. In addition, much of the waste we are generating is not recycled and is thus accumulating.

Even if new technologies could enlarge and conserve the planet's carrying capacity, obsolete technologies and unreflective practices are reducing it. This is a recipe for trouble. The critical shortages that develop do not just lead to a decrease in the material standard of living of the less privileged populations: they lead to sudden ruptures in the entire interdependent world system — to extensive famines, massive migrations, and spreading epidemics. These are likely to produce social and political conflict, unrest and chaos, criminality and warfare. The unfolding of the two basic trends will impact on the life and future of all people, worldwide.

The unfolding trends

The basic trends are obvious if we look at two of the essential resources of human existence: water and soil. Both water and soil are renewable resources, but both are under pressure. Their rate of consumption exceeds their rate of renewal.

At first glance, the idea of a worldwide water squeeze seems improbable. After all, four-fifths of the planet's surface is water. Water for human use has to be fresh, however, and the salt water in the oceans and seas makes up 97.5 per cent of the planet's total water volume. Two-thirds of the remainder is concentrated in the polar icecaps, and underground. The renewable fresh water potentially available for human consumption — in lakes, rivers, and reservoirs — is no more than 0.007 per cent of the water on the surface of the Earth.

In the past, this relatively thin trickle was more than enough to satisfy human needs. Even in 1950, there was a potential annual supply of some $17,000m^3$ of fresh water for every woman, man, and child. However, since the rate of water withdrawal has been more than double the rate of population growth, by 1995 this amount had decreased to $7,500m^3$. If current trends were to continue, in the year 2025 there would be only $5,100m^3$ of water available per person per year. This would create serious water shortages in many parts of the world. North Africa, the Middle East, India and Central Asia would feel the brunt of the impact, but parts of Eastern Europe, Mexico, and the United States would also suffer its effects.

Currently, a third of the world's peoples experience serious problems in accessing good quality fresh water, while two-thirds still have an adequate supply. These proportions would reverse by the year 2025. In that year the amount of fresh water withdrawable with available technology, and at acceptable cost, would be merely a third of that taken out in 1950.

Experts at the World Health Organization, the World Meteorological Organization, the UN Environment Programme and UNESCO foresee that by the middle of the next decade there will be serious local and regional water emergencies. On the world level, by the year 2030 the descending supply curve will intersect the ascending demand curve. This will create unlivable conditions for more than two-thirds of the human population. And, without the shadow of a doubt, it will also create serious social and political conflicts, massive migrations, spreading epidemics, and widespread environmental degradation.

Soil poses a similar problem. With the exception of sandy deserts and high mountains, the surface of the continents is covered with soil. But soil of a quality suitable for agriculture is relatively scarce. It takes nature from 100 to 400 years to create just 10 millimeters of productive topsoil; to build a layer of 30 centimeters takes any-where from three to twelve thousand years. The UN's Food and Agriculture Organization estimates that there are 3,031 million hectares (about 7,490 million acres) of cropland currently available, 71 per cent of them in the developing world. This is a precious resource, desperately needed to cover the food and agricultural needs of a growing human population. Yet pressures of human activity produce erosion; destructuring; compaction; impoverish-ment; excessive desiccation; the accumulation of toxic salts; the leaching of nutritious elements, and urban and industrial pollution. For the past few decades these processes have resulted in the loss of five to seven million hectares (twelve to seventeen million acres) of cropland per year. If human activity pressures are not relieved, between 20 and 30 per cent of the planet's topsoil will be lost by the beginning of the third millennium. This would critically reduce the world's food and agricultural production.

Keeping an equilibrium between humanity's demand and the planet's supply, whether of water, soil, air, energy, or raw materi-als, depends on the kind of technologies we use and the demands we make. Long-term sustainability is determined not by how many people use the resources, but how much they use per head.

If all people lived like Lucy — the African hominid that is said to be the common ancestor of modern man — the planet could sup-port fifty or a hundred billion people, considerably more than the population we now have, or are likely to have in the foreseeable future. But people today do not live like Lucy: they live like the 'Ngo family in Nigeria; the Singh family in India; the Ito family in Japan; the Leonhard family in Germany, and the Jones family in America. Lucy used perhaps two liters of water a day for drinking but, while modern people still need that amount for bodily health, the Itos, Leonhards, and Joneses use another six liters for cooking, and over 80 liters for washing and flushing the toilet. This does not include the 87 per cent of the water consumed currently that goes into irrigation, and the further share devoted to industrial uses and water-borne sanitation.

Lucy did not consume energy beyond her own muscles and the forces available in nature, but the 'Ngos use half a kilowatt hour of commercial electrical energy, the Singhs several KWhs, and the Itos, Leonhards and Joneses up to 8 KWh. The planet could support ten or perhaps fifteen billion people living like the 'Ngos and the Singhs, but six billion people living like the Joneses is out of the question. A child born to the Joneses consumes two or three dozen times more resources than a child born to the Singhs, and several hundred times more resources than one born to the 'Ngos. In the eighty-plus years of his or her expected lifespan, Mr or Ms Jones will consume 800,000 kilowatts of electrical energy; 2,500,000 liters of water; 21,000 tons of gasoline; 220,000 kilos of steel; the wood of one thousand trees, and generate 60 tons of municipal waste. With current technologies and at acceptable cost, the planet could hardly sustain more than two billion people living at their level.

Critical choices

There are critical choices before us. To continue to augment our own material standard of living means foreclosing the chance of other people to augment theirs. We must find alternatives. These cannot be aimed at reducing the basic resource use of poor people — improving the material basis of life is essential for those who live at or near the lower limits of physical subsistence. If all these masses, the great majority of whom live in Sub-Saharan Africa and South Asia, are not to be condemned to death through feebleness, disease, thirst, and hunger, economic and ecological conditions must be created under which they can increase their use of habitable space, food, forests, water, air, basic raw materials, and energy, and obtain the minimum of education that is a precondition of life in a complex world.

Currently, there are 1.3 billion people on the planet living below the absolute poverty line. In villages and towns, and in the shantytowns surrounding cities, they attempt to obtain the resources to meet their basic needs from nature. This is becoming increasingly difficult. Mining and other extractive industries have degraded many of the originally rich ecosystems, and rapid population growth has made for an overexploitation of the existing resources. In many areas of Africa, Central Asia, and the Indian subcontinent women and children now spend on average four to six hours searching for fuelwood, and as long drawing and carrying water. In consequence poor people are fleeing their native towns and villages, searching for a better life — or just any life — in the cities.

According to the UN High Commission for Refugees, one in every 17 people today is a refugee. The number of landless, jobless, and homeless people is estimated at 500 million. At the same time urban complexes are growing: one out of every three people lives in a city. By the year 2025, two out of every three are expected to do so. If these trends continue, by that year there will be more than 500 cities with populations of over one million, and thirty megacities exceeding eight million. Cities, already fatally overstressed, will not be able to absorb this human load.

Life at the subsistence level is degrading both for human beings and for the environment. While people suffer from malnutrition, joblessness, and inhuman living conditions, the productive lands are overworked, rivers and lakes are contaminated, and water tables are drawn down. Evidently, current pressures on nature and human habitation could be reduced if poor people were to have smaller families. But in the absence of inhuman measures, massive reductions in family size are hardly possible. Poverty encourages high fertility rates — children help subsistence families garner the resources needed for survival. In consequence some 90 per cent of the current population increase (about 90 million persons per year) occurs in the poor countries and regions of the world.

World poverty is not a stable and stationary condition: it constantly aggravates itself. Above all, it is aggravated by conditions over which poor people have no control: the workings of the world economy. The international economic system is pushing more and more people from traditional, relatively stable patterns of rural existence into abject, self- and environment-destroying poverty. According to the UN Development Programme's Human Development Report, since 1980 some 15 developing countries have known surging economic growth, but 100 experienced stagnation or decline, spelling lower incomes for 1.6 billion people. In 70 of the negative growth countries the average income is less today than it was in 1980; in 43 of them, less than in 1970.

Poor populations in the developing world cannot expect much from their national economies: they are beset by "structural" problems. The price of the commodities many of them export have fallen (due to a raw-material glut produced by worldwide infrastructure development), but the price of manufactured goods has not. As a result the majority of the developing world economies suffer from worsening terms of trade — they have less export income to cover their growing import bills. As domestic needs go up and national purchasing power declines, the indebtedness of the countries increases. The developing world's debt overhang is now 1.2 trillion US dollars — nearly half of the developing countries' joint GNP. Owing to new loans, and debt servicing on current ones, there is a net "reverse transfer" of wealth estimated at some 40 billion dollars a year from the developing world to the lender banks of the industrialized countries and the financial institutions of the international community.

The economic trend is unmistakable: it is in the direction of a widening gap between rich and poor countries, and between rich and poor people within the countries. The rich get richer still. The net worth of the 358 billionaires of this world — of which 88 are in the poor countries — is about 760 billion US dollars. This is equivalent to the net worth of more than 2.5 billion people, over 40 per cent of the world population. The income distribution in contemporary France is about as unequal as it was on the eve of the French Revolution and in England it is worse than it was at the end of the 19th century. In 1990 the richest 20 per cent earned 85 per cent of the global income (in 1960, it earned "only" 70 per cent), while the share of the poorest 20 per cent fell to 1.7 per cent (it was 2.3 per cent in 1960). Today, the poorest 20 per cent receive 1.4 per cent of the global income, and the next poorest 1.9 per cent. In the last 30 years, the ratio of inequality in the world has doubled.

A first conclusion

The big picture deserves to be better known and taken to heart. All people, especially people in the industrialized world, need to face facts and understand the consequences. The first reaction is often to delegate the blame to the poor countries. This is neither ethical nor reasonable. Unless their people perish of malnutrition, or their governments sterilize their young, their numbers will still grow and their resource use will increase. Even so, the great majority of them could never keep up, or even catch up, with the Joneses.

We must consider a better option: reducing the load we place on the planet's resources and life-support systems. In this matter the people who are relatively well-off have the decisive say. Poor people must obtain food, housing, jobs, and some necessary minimum of education — other than reducing their family size, there is little they or anybody could do to cut back on their basic resource use. Above the level of basic needs, human choices multiply. There is more than one way the Joneses could live, and indeed live well: a high quality of life does not necessarily mean a high material standard of living. On the contrary, a high level of consumption can soon turn unhealthy and produce well-known illnesses of civilization — hypertension, stroke, heart disease, cancer, and the equally well-known pollution of air, water, and land. Many studies and surveys show that one can decrease the material standard of one's living at the same time as increasing the quality of one's life.

Affluent lifestyles are admired and emulated. Because the Joneses drive a private car to work, shopping, and recreation, and make use of it even when public transport is available, the vast masses of the developing countries want to own and use cars for much the same reasons and same purposes. China, with some 1.2 billion people, is already on the way to realizing this ambition. In the center of the "miracle city" Shenzhen in the South, there are hardly any bicycles left, while private cars, including luxury models, abound — together with traffic jams and air pollution. Because the Joneses eat steaks and hamburgers and feed much of the produce of agricultural lands to domestic animals and household pets, people in the developing countries aspire to the same kind of luxury — hamburger stands and fast-food restaurants are ubiquitous even in the poorest countries. And because the Joneses power their homes and factories with electricity derived from fossil fuels or nuclear reactors, the Singhs and the 'Ngos want to have their own share of these resources, even if they are nonrenewable and polluting, or unsafe under local conditions.

Suppose that the Joneses — and the Leonhards and the Itos — decide to grow the responsible way. Would that really make a difference to the wellbeing of the Singhs and the 'Ngos? It is very likely that it would. The key factor could prove to be the example they provide: in our globally networked world it could spread nearly instantly to the five continents. Responsible lifestyles would spread, and that would be in everyone's interest. Using clean and renewable sources of energy, living closer to nature, eating fresh produce, walking more and using public transport are not sacrifices: they are healthier than sitting in cars in overcrowded streets, suffering from cholesterol and high blood pressure, and breathing polluted air.

There is a better way to live — and to produce and consume. It is time to discard the inherited model of wellbeing and create a model that can be responsibly adopted in the West, and creatively adapted in the rest.

CHAPTER 2

CAN WE CHANGE DIRECTION?

An ancient Chinese proverb warns, "If we do not change the direction in which we are moving, we are likely to end up exactly where we are headed." Applied to contemporary humanity, this would be disastrous. If we keep moving in the direction we are moving we may become a threat to all life on the planet. If we do not change direction we are on the way to continued overpopulation; spreading poverty; increasing militarization; accelerating climate change; growing food and energy shortages; worsening industrial, urban, and agricultural pollution of air, water, and soil; a further destruction of the ozone layer; accelerating reduction of biodiversity; continued loss of atmospheric oxygen; a growing threat of large-scale catastrophes due to nuclear accident and nuclear waste, and of smaller-scale but possibly widespread disasters through the accumulation of toxins in soil, air, and water and toxic additives in food and drink.

Continuing as we are will lead to a world with serious shortages of food, water, energy, and other resources; a changed climate; double the current population; rural starvation; urban breakdown, and increasing disparity between rich and poor with growing levels of conflict, crime, and violence. None of this is fate but depends on choices we can make.

We *could* change direction, in principle. There are life-conserving and enhancing alternatives to every life-threatening or depressing process. Among the most obvious examples, we could:

• Reduce emissions of CO_2 and other greenhouse gases into the atmosphere;

• Reforest denuded lands and prevent erosion of cultivable lands;

• Reduce and clean up pollution;

• Develop alternative fuels;

• Do away with weapons of mass destruction and dangerous technologies;

• Reduce the gap between the rich and the poor;

• Inhibit conspicuous consumption;

• Provide better living and working conditions for women;

• Encourage a reverse flow of people from the cities back to the countryside;

• Retrain the unemployed and the underemployed;

• Facilitate environment-friendly business ventures;

• Reallocate resources in favor of education and health care;

• Encourage smaller families.

Courses of action capable of moving us in a more constructive direction are known. In its 1995 report, the Commission on Global Governance put forward a number of achievable recommendations for enhancing international security, promoting global cooperation, managing economic interdependence, and strengthening the rule of law. The Commission concluded that it is not a question of the capacity to take the required actions, but a question of the will to take them. In turn, The World Game Institute recently estimated that a quarter of the world's military expenditures could prevent soil erosion; stop ozone depletion; stabilize population; prevent global warming and acid rain; provide clean safe energy, and water; provide shelter; eliminate illiteracy, malnutrition and starvation, and reduce the debt of the developing nations. Even small reductions in military spending could fund major health and literacy programs, create essential infrastructures, and bring marginalized people into the ambit of the modern world economy. But such "peace dividends," like measures for global security and cooperation, though known and discussed, are not implemented: they are not priorities on the international agenda.

Will is similarly lacking with regard to the environment. On the one hand our world is relieved of the specter of superpower confrontation while on the other it is threatened by ecological collapse, yet the world's governments spend one thousand billion dollars a year on arms and the military while — notwithstanding promises and declarations made at the Rio Summit — only a tiny fraction of that sum is spent on ensuring a livable environment. We *could* change direction, but as of now we do not.

A Neolithic illusion

The values and beliefs that created today's trends were not born yesterday. Long-term trends overshadow our present and threaten our future, their roots go back to the beginnings of history. Conditions under which humans lived on this planet at the dawning of the Neolithic era some 10,000 years ago were fundamentally different from those in which we now find ourselves, yet the values and beliefs those conditions gave rise to are in some ways still with us. Our technologies and our ways of life have evolved, but our values and perceptions have not kept pace.

The decisive difference between conditions of life in modern and traditional societies doubtless lies in the relationship of humans to nature. For 99 per cent of the five million years since our ancestors descended from the trees, human communities lived in a closed system with their natural environment. Only the energy of the sun entered this system, and only the heat radiated into space left it — everything else was cycled and recycled within it. Food and water came from the local environment and they were returned into that environment and recycled. Even in death the human body did not leave the ecological system: it entered the soil and contributed to its fertility. Nothing that men and women brought into being ever accumulated as "non-biodegradable" toxins; nothing they did caused any lasting damage to nature's cycles of generation and regeneration.

The situation changed when groups of early humans learned to manipulate their environment. Though at first human bands and tribes did not poison their land, air, and water, the load they placed on their immediate milieu began to increase. When the control of fire permitted the stocking of perishable food over longer periods and allowed people to congregate further from their food supply, human communities grew in number. They extended over the continents and began to transform nature to fit their needs. Our ancestors were no longer content merely to gather their food; they learned to hunt, and then to plant seeds and use rivers for irrigation and the removal of wastes. They domesticated some species of dogs, horses, and cattle. These practices enabled them to extend their dominion over vaster territories, but also increased their impact. Nourishment flowed from a purposively modified environment, and the growing wastes from larger and technologically more sophisticated communities disappeared conveniently, with smoke vanishing into thin air, and solid waste washing downstream in rivers and dispersing in the seas.

Nature seemed to be effectively open: the environment appeared to be an infinite source of goods and an infinite sink of wastes. Even when a local milieu suffered — from the excessive cutting down of trees and working of soils, for example — there were virgin lands to conquer and to exploit. But where virgin territories were not available, overexploited environments would often collapse. Easter Island is a dramatic example.

A remote piece of land, 2000 miles from South America and 1600 miles from the nearest inhabited Pacific island, Easter Island was settled by Polynesians about 1600 years ago. At that time it was a pristine paradise with subtropical forests, many species of birds, and no major predators. The settlers prospered; they developed a complex economic and political system, and a sophisticated culture. Emulating the stone carvings of their forebears, they erected larger and larger statues, trying to surpass each other in sheer size and virtuosity.

The number of settlers grew steadily, eventually reaching perhaps as many as 20,000. They used the forest cover for fuel, canoes and houses, and for the rollers and rope for transporting the giant stone heads of their statues. For centuries, islanders increased their numbers and enjoyed peace and prosperity. But a time came when the trees were cut down quicker than they could regenerate. The scarcity of wood for seagoing canoes reduced the size of the fish catch, so people turned to local birds and animals to supplement their diet. Then soil erosion and deforestation diminished their crop yields, and soon the island could no longer feed its human population. The evidence, reconstructed by anthropologist Jared Diamond, suggests that disorder ensued. The ruling class was overthrown, and as clan fought clan they toppled and desecrated each other's giant statues. By Easter Sunday of 1772, when the Europeans arrived, the once-fertile tropical paradise was a barren and desolate piece of land. Remaining inhabitants lived in a state of permanent hunger, violence, and cannibalism.

Elsewhere, environmental limits were not overstepped so obviously and drastically. Traditional peoples were stability-oriented; they revered nature and the ways of life of their ancestors more than new tools and new practices. They looked after their life-support systems and used only as much as nature could supply and regenerate. Of course, there were also innovation-oriented civilizations, and these tended to overexploit their environment — the Mycenean and the Olmec civilizations, and those of the Indus Valley are notable examples. On the continents the environment was vast and generous. Plants and animals could be domesticated, and larger and larger human settlements could evolve. If forests were chopped down quicker than they could regenerate, and if soils were overexploited and impoverished, people could move on. If a particular community collapsed in one place, another community came to flower somewhere else.

In the Levant an innovation-oriented community arose. Here, at the birthplace of Western civilization, the inventiveness of the human spirit was not content with adapting itself to the eternal rhythms and perennial cycles of nature, but sought ways to harness these rhythms and cycles to serve human ends. The land, though hot and arid in spots, appeared amenable to exploitation. Of course, even here the domination of nature exacted a price. In Sumer, for example, existence for the early settlers was harsh: flash floods washed away irrigation channels and dams, and when they dried up they left fields arid. Not surprisingly, in the Sumerian belief system man was the gods' slave. Gods created humans because they themselves did not want to toil in the fields. Sumerian statues pictured bowed people, with frightened eyes and prayerful hands. By contrast the environment of the Nile was more benign. The great river irrigated the land, brought in silt and washed away wastes with dependable regularity. It made for easy travel downstream, while the prevailing winds from the Mediterranean allowed good sailing upstream.

The subsequent course of Western civilization was shaped by the cultures and ambitions pioneered in the Levant, but more by Hellenic and Hebraic than Sumerian and Egyptian influences. The Hellenic and the Hebraic ways were distinct also from each other — Greek mythology presented a sharp contrast to the belief system of the Jews. Greek gods were pagan deities; there were many of them and they personified every human appetite, including sexual drives both normal and aberrant. They were said to have regular concourse, and intercourse, with humans, and their behavior was believed to be licentious even among themselves — Hera, Zeus' spouse, connived to seduce her husband into plots he would later regret while Aphrodite, the wife of Hephaistos, slept with Mars.

In contrast with the human-like gods and goddesses of the Greeks, Jahweh, the god of the Jews, was a jealous and morally exacting god. Unlike the Greek gods who demanded virtuosity, Jahweh demanded virtue of His people: strict adherence to His Covenant, meaning no worship of other gods and idols, and strict obedience to a code of behavior with categorical distinctions between right and wrong. The discipline imposed by the strict ethics of the Jews proved more enduring than the permissive attitude of the Greeks. In the form it was later given by Jesus, the proclaimed Messiah to whom many Jews as well as Romans converted, the Jewish belief system weathered the rise and fall of the Roman empire.

The Judeo-Christian religion created a closer relationship between humans and their one God, and a more distant relationship between humans and their natural environment. Man was held to be the only species created in the image of God, the only Being with an eternal soul worthy of salvation. The Book of Genesis ordered Adam and Eve and their descendants to "be fruitful and multiply, and replenish the Earth and subdue it; and have dominion over the fish of the sea and the fowl in the air, and over every living thing that moveth upon the Earth." Obeying the divine injunction to dominate the environment brought tangible results; it enabled ever larger populations to exploit ever more of the planet's resources. While in the East Hinduism, Lao Tse and the Buddha taught that human communities and habitats are an integral part of nature, in the West people labored earnestly to master the Earth and make it serve them.

Subduing the Earth, as the experience of the Easter Islanders and the Sumerians testifies, was often a two-edged sword. It created food and livelihood for an increasing population, but at the same time it also denuded forested lands and produced an arid environment visited by floods and other natural disasters. The growth of human domination over nature expressed, as well as resulted from, the development of a culture that divested itself from the conservatism of traditional societies. As Western monotheism took hold, people separated the images of their deities from nature, replacing animal and ancestral spirits, goddesses of fertility and of the Earth with august male gods such as Aton, Jehovah, and Allah. They began to look on the natural world as a creation of a transcendent God — a creation He undertook mainly for the benefit of His people. The new heroes were not shamans who would teach how to imitate nature and safeguard its cycles, but charismatic leaders who would change the environment for the glory of their people. Will and ambition, rather than nature, suggested "the way." Humans became co-creators of history.

Such were the roots of the individualism that arose in the West. It created a profound schism between man and nature, between self and other, and mind and matter. In the course of recent centuries, the human being came to be seen as separate from, and indeed superior to, the natural orders. Nature has been relegated to being a source of food and a place of recreation. In our day jet airplanes, computers, air-conditioned high-rise office buildings, antibiotics, telecommunications, and mass-produced grain and poultry provide seemingly tangible support for belief in man's superiority. Modern man (and regarding Western male-dominated civilization the masculine pronoun is not misplaced) left the all-encompassing womb of nature to live in a universe of his own creation. He succeeded in wrenching, in Francis Bacon's phrase, the secrets of nature from her womb for his own benefit.

Throughout the modern age, Western man has been intent on using nature for his own benefit, empowered by technology and encouraged by the protestant ethic of hard work. While the advantages have been obvious, the drawbacks have been less so. Chemically-bolstered mechanized agriculture has made soils yield more produce per acre, and made more acres available for produce, but it has also increased the growth of algae and choked lakes and waterways. Chemicals such as DDT proved effective insecticides, but they also poisoned entire animal, bird, and insect populations. The material consumption of city populations has created masses of garbage that have threatened the health of their own inhabitants. For over three centuries the apparent success of Western technological civilization obscured the fact that its life-supporting environment was increasingly exposed to more and more stress.

The Neolithic illusion of an open and infinite ecological system was maintained as long as nature offered unexploited resources and unfilled sinks. But today, at the end of the 20th century, such an illusion has inevitably shattered: the impact created by nearly six billion humans is hard to ignore. Contemporary people no longer make fires just to cook their food and heat their dwellings: they fire powerful steel-mills and electrical generators. They no longer discard just their household wastes into the environment: they inject tens of thousands of chemical compounds into land, river, and sea; dump millions of tons of sludge and solid waste into the oceans; release billions of tons of CO_2 into the air, and raise the level of radioactivity in water, land, as well as the atmosphere.

The wastes discarded into the environment do not vanish but come back to plague those who produced them — and their neighbors near and far. The refuse dumped into the sea does not dissipate in an endless expanse of water but returns to poison marine life and infest coastal regions. In the rich countries some one million chemicals produced by industry are bubbling through the groundwater systems; in poor countries rivers and lakes have up to a hundred times the accepted level of pollutants. In the late 1980s the water in Malaysia's Kelang river had enough mercury to function as pesticide. Even the smoke rising from homesteads and factories fails to dissolve and disappear: the CO_2 released by it remains in the atmosphere and interferes with the world's weather.

The Neolithic illusion is a myth, and when myths become misleading, they fade and vanish. In Central America dozens of Mayan temples lie abandoned; in Peru countless Incan monuments are scattered in ruins; there are Celtic cairns in Wales, Khmer statues in Kampuchea, Sumerian ziggurats in Iraq, and giant stone heads in Easter Island — mute witnesses of once flowering myths that disappeared, either because they misguided their people, or because more viable myths and cultures appeared in their milieu. The Neolithic illusion — the myth of an infinitely open environment — must disappear as well: it has become a threat to the whole of humanity.

Modern-day myths

Julius Caesar wrote that men willingly believe what they wish. What they wish is often what influential peers or persuasive leaders believe; what they were brought up to believe by their parents and schools; what fills their emotional needs; what produces easy answers; or simply what most others believe. Popular beliefs are seldom reached by deep-seated soul-searching and an impassioned review of the evidence.

The fact that myths abound in modern societies is in itself neither wrong nor surprising. As anthropologist Joseph Campbell noted, myths serve to explain the external world; guide individual development; provide social direction; and address spiritual questions. They combine what people know, and what they hope for and desire, into maps that guide them through the choices of a lifetime. Myths must provide choices that enable a people to survive and develop, otherwise they become a threat to the society that maintains them. The modern mythology has become a threat: it has not kept up with people's ways of life and society's organizational forms, technologies, and environmental impacts.

The myths that fail

• Order through hierarchy: Order can only be achieved by rules and laws and their proper enforcement, and this requires a chain of command that is recognized and obeyed by all. A few people at the top — mostly males — make up the rules, legislate the laws, and give the orders to ensure compliance with them. All others have to obey the rules and take their places within the established social and political order.

• The separateness of individuals: When all is said and done we are all separate individuals enclosed by our skin and pursuing our own interests; everyone has only himself or herself to rely on. The same goes for our country: it, too, is a separate entity, defined by its borders and has only itself — its leaders and its folk — to rely upon.

• The ideology of Westphalia: the formally constituted nation-state is the sole political reality, the only entity with true sovereignty — as the legal conventions that came into force at the Peace of Westphalia specified. Groups and communities within the nation-state are intrinsic parts of it, without sovereignty of their own. And groupings and alliances that go above or beyond the nation-state, even if formed by national governments, are temporary pragmatic measures, in force only as long as they serve the perceived interests of the governments that created them.

• The reversibility of current problems: Our problems are only temporary; they are but an interlude of perturbations after which everything will go back to normal. All we need to do is manage the current difficulties, using tried and tested methods of problem solving — and, when necessary, crisis management. Business as unusual has evolved out of business as usual, and sooner or later will reverse back into it.

The real situation

Such outdated beliefs have failed, and are rapidly turning dangerous.

• Male-dominated hierarchies may work in the Army, but they do not work even in the structures of the Church, much less in business and in society. Leading managers have already learned the advantages of lean structures and teamwork, but most social and political institutions today still operate in traditional hierarchical mode. As a result they tend to be heavy-handed, their workings cumbersome and inefficient.

• Seeing ourselves as separate from the social and the natural world in which we live threatens to convert natural impulses to ensure our own interests into a short-sighted struggle among ever more desperate and unequal competitors. It is conducive to the irresponsible use — and abuse — of human labor and the environment.

• Admitting nothing but our own nation-state as the focus of allegiance is a mistaken form of patriotism. It leads to chauvinism and intolerance, perilously held in check by international trade agreements and political alliances.

• No experience of problems and crises can change these perceptions if we remain convinced that the problems we encounter are but temporary disturbances in an unchanging and perhaps unchangeable *status quo*.

Mistaken premises

A number of mistaken premises underlie these modern-day myths:

• The law of the jungle: Life is a struggle for survival. Be aggressive or you perish.

• My country, right or wrong: The international environment is also a jungle. National interests must be strongly defended.

• A rising tide lifts all boats: If as a nation we grow and prosper, all our citizens will benefit, the poorest included.

• The trickle-down theory: Another watery metaphor, it holds that wealth is bound to "trickle-down" from the rich to the poor. The more wealth there is at our rich-country top, the greater the trickle that reaches the poor-country bottom.

• The invisible hand: Formulated by Adam Smith, it holds that individual and social interests are automatically harmonized. If I do well for myself, I benefit my community.

• The self-regulating economy: A justification for trust in the invisible hand, it tells us that if we ensure perfect competition in a market system, the benefits will be properly allocated by that system without need for further intervention.

• The cult of efficiency: We should get the maximum out of every person, every machine and every organization. The end product, and whether or not it is useful, is not a major concern.

• The technological imperative: Anything that can be done must be done. If it can be made or performed it can be sold, and if it is sold it is good for us and the economy.

• Economic rationality: The value of everything, including human beings, can be calculated in money. What everybody wants is to get rich, the rest is idle conversation or simple pretense.

• The future is none of our business: Why should we worry about the good of the next generation—after all, *we* had to fend for ourselves. The next generation will just have to do the same. Modern man, it appears, struggles for survival in a jungle, is ready to go and fight for his country because his country must survive in the international jungle, benefits others by his own pursuit of material gain, trusts invisible forces to right wrongs, worships efficiency, is ready to make, sell and consume practically anything, dismisses things that are not calculable in money or do not have immediate payoffs, and loves his children but is indifferent to the conditions it bequeathes to their generation. This is a strange rationality, and acting by it no longer pays off.

Why our myths have failed

• Belief in the law of the jungle encourages tooth-and claw competition that fails to make use of the benefits of cooperation — a vital factor in an interdependent world.

• The chauvinistic assertion "my country, right or wrong" plays untold havoc within and between countries throughout the world. It calls for people to go and fight for causes which their country later repudiates; to espouse values and worldviews of a small group of political leaders, and to ignore growing cultural, social, and economic ties evolving among people in different parts of the globe.

• Holding to the dogmas of the rising tide, the trickle-down effect and the invisible hand, promote selfish behavior in the comforting — but certainly no longer warranted — belief that this is bound to benefit others.

• Faith in a perfectly self-regulating market ignores the fact that market mechanisms only function well when the playing field is level; when it is not, the players on the high ground distort its operations in their own favor. They dominate the market, and push less powerful players to the margins.

• Efficiency, without regard to what is produced and whom it will benefit, leads to the catering to the demands of the affluent and the neglect of the needs of the poor. It polarizes society into privileged and disenfranchised segments.

• Following the technological imperative becomes an unaffordable luxury at a time when economic growth curves slacken, markets become saturated, the environment approaches the limits of its pollution absorption capacity, and energy and material resources become scarce and expensive. It results in a plethora of goods that people only think they need. People use some of them at their peril as they are actually wasteful, damaging to health, polluting, alienating, or stress-provoking.

• The naive reduction of everything and everybody to economic value may have seemed rational in epochs when a great economic upswing turned all heads and pushed all other things into the background, but is foolhardy at a time when people are rediscovering social and spiritual values and opting for natural foods, environmentally friendly products, and lifestyles of voluntary simplicity.

• And living without conscious forward planning — though it may have worked in days of rapid growth when everything had a way of panning out — is not a responsible option at a time when critical choices have to be made with profound and possibly irreversible consequences for ourselves and the next generations.

We have long outgrown the conditions under which our ancestors lived for millions of years. We have outgrown even the conditions under which our own fathers and grandfathers lived for most of this century. Yet we still persist in the Neolithic illusion of an infinite and inexhaustible environment, and in modern myths that justify and legitimize the blind and relentless pursuit of individual, institutional, and national self-interest.

The old myths no longer give us reliable guidance, yet we let ourselves be guided by them. The direction in which they are taking us is highly dangerous; continuing on this path is not in any of our best interests.

PART TWO

THE NEW IMPERATIVES

On 31st August 1997, Diana Princess of Wales and her consort entered a Mercedes car behind the Ritz hotel in Paris to seek privacy elsewhere. They were pursued by sensation-hungry paparazzi, and their driver, wishing to shake them off, sped through the streets of the city. His control impaired by alcohol, he rammed the pillar of an underpass and a spectacular accident killed Diana, her consort, and himself. For the first half of September, the international news media made the story of the accident, of the funeral, and the reactions of the British royal family into the world's principal item of public interest.

Almost a decade previously, on 7th October 1988, Ahmaogak, an Eskimo hunter searching for bow-head whales off the north coast of Alaska, discovered three California grey whales gasping for air through a rapidly closing hole in the ice. He reported this to friends in the local wildlife management office, and from there the news leaked to the media. This event triggered "Operation Breakout" in which the United States, the Soviet Union, two corporations, Greenpeace, and two private individuals spent almost six million US dollars to free the whales. 150 journalists, including 20 TV networks from four continents, covered the story. Each day more than a billion people watched it on television, and further billions followed it on the pages of printed media[1].

These two seemingly disparate events have more in common than it may appear. Both indicate widespread interest on the part of the media and the public in sensational news stories, and this interest does have a positive aspect. Interest in Diana was more than interest in a controversial member of a royal family: it was also interest in someone who gained the sympathy of thousands of millions through her personality and the time and energy she spent on deserving causes. Interest in the whales showed empathy with the fate of intelligent beings of other species.

Yet the fascination of the global media and world public with these cases has a shadow side: it occurs to the exclusion of reports that would have equal claim on our attention. Between 8th and 28th October 1986, while the world watched the saga of the whales, half a million children died of malnutrition; 1.5 billion tons of topsoil and 2,300 square miles of tropical rainforest were lost; the human population increased by five million, and the world's governments spent 60 billion US dollars on arms and the military. During the first two weeks in September 1997, much the same occurred: the fateful curves of global resource availability and human resource demand evolved at an accelerated rate. But though this development has a critical impact on everyone's life and future, it escaped the world's attention.

Such myopia about the trends that decide our destiny is not responsible. Local and global events of our day need to be viewed more meaningfully. The public has a right to know the big picture, and its ramifications for our life. It is not reasonable to induce people to take more interest in the fate of royalty, or some animals, not to mention the features of a new car, the activities of a movie star or the score of a football game, rather than in the growth-rate of populations, the evolution of cities, the contamination of the environment and the safety of nuclear wastes. The people of the world have to realize that we must act to head off the blind continuation of the exponential growth of our use and abuse of the planet's available resources, and the reduction of the planet's humanly relevant carrying capacity. In addition to whatever fascinating stories come about, media and public attention must not fail to focus on today's decisive trends, and on the urgent need creatively to evolve the patterns of thought and action that dominate our existence. It has become imperative that:

- *Individuals think globally and live responsibly*
- *Businesses evolve a new enterprise culture*
- *Politics lift the sights of national governments*
- *Society adopt a code for environmental morality*
- *Peoples and states create a culture of interexistence.*

CHAPTER 3

THINKING GLOBALLY, LIVING RESPONSIBLY

We are getting used to questioning our prospects for the future, but we seldom think the questions through. We ask, for example, whether it is wise to allow jobs to flow out of our country and large masses of people to flow in. We question the wisdom of environmentally "unfriendly" practices and the safety of large-scale technological installations, whether conventional or nuclear. And we also question whether the kind of growth we experienced in the 70s and 80s could be continued in the 90s and beyond. But other than a few visionaries, we do not question whether we not only could, but actually *should*, change the course we have set for ourselves in the past.

When such questions crop up, we tend to shift the responsibility — or the blame — onto others. Not us: leaders in politics and business should be entrusted to cope with today's problems and chart our way toward the future. No doubt, people in leadership positions do have a major share of responsibility for our destiny, but we must not forget that we, too, ordinary citizens, consumers, and members of social, ethnic, and business communities have responsibilities; we, too, have an important role to play.

A role for the individual

Just how important is our role? What can one individual do to mold the shape of things to come? As Mahatma Gandhi said: "if you want to change the world, change yourself". In today's turbulent and information-penetrated environment fads and fashions, news of wars and catastrophes, and the activities of political figures and movie stars spread like wildfire. Alternative patterns of thinking and behaving could spread just as well.

In the 5th century BC, the Chinese sage Lao Tse noted, "One individual's life serves as an example for other individuals; one's family serves as a model for other families; one's community serves as a standard for other communities; one's state serves as a measure for other states; and one's country serves as an ideal for all countries."

In today's information-penetrated and globalized world, the ancient wisdom of the Tao acquires fresh pertinence. What I do as an individual can inform other individuals; what my family does can reach other families, and what my community, state, and country does can be known, and perhaps emulated, by other communities, states, and countries. These possibilities exist and need to be taken seriously. Margaret Mead has put it well: "Never doubt the power of a small group of committed people to change the world; in fact, nothing else ever has."

Global thinking

If you want to change the world, or just your neighborhood, a good bet is to gain the commitment of those around you. And the best bet is start with yourself. Commit yourself — to what? There are two simple rules of thumb we can all follow.

The first rule is to think globally. Thinking in appropriate and adapted ways is a uniquely human capability. The higher animals can also learn by experience, but their basic behavior remains guided by instinct — and instinct cannot be changed except by the slow processes of mutation and natural selection. The dominance of experience over instinct is what distinguishes the faster cultural evolution of humans from the slower genetic evolution of animals. We can learn from experience, and our conscious assessment of experience can steer and transcend our inherited instincts. Global thinking is the fruit of learning from the experience of living and acting in today's globalized and information-imbued societies.

The benefit of global thinking is not to obtain a catalog of ready-made blueprints for making proper choices in any and all circumstances; rather, it is to acquire the perspective by which we can make wise choices of our own. Global thinking is not thinking in vague and general categories, nor in millions and billions — whether of humans, hectares, or barrels of oil. It is thinking in terms of processes rather than structures, in terms of dynamic wholes rather than static parts. Global thinking means seeing the forest, and not just the trees.

A person who fails to think globally sees only the trees — for example, those of Brazil. He sees the trees of the rainforest, and Brazil's government in need of foreign exchange. He also sees bulldozer operators and ranchers in need of work, a transporter in need of cargo, and hamburger franchises in need of meat. A globally thinking person sees the whole picture. He sees that the disappearance of trees in the rainforest triggers the loss of topsoil which leads to changing weather patterns which in turn lead to advancing deserts and loss of oxygen. He realizes this creates a vicious cycle that ends by destroying itself, and everything connected with it.

For a globally thinking person waste and pollution, whatever its form, are not merely irritating and irrational: they are emotionally unacceptable. If we use narrow and short-term reasoning to assess impacts and effects, we will not be upset at a plastic bag thrown out of a speeding car or left behind at a picnic spot or at the beach; we will find arguments for the economy of clean-up and the tolerance of limited pollution. But when we think globally, we will feel the acute pain of pollution and waste, and will be unable to countenance them.

Global thinking extends to everything we do and all we consume. It extends to the choice of the food we eat. A globally thinking person grasps that a red meat diet indulges a personal fancy at the expense of resources essential for the human family. Meat comes from cattle, and cattle require feedstuff to live. The grain fed to cattle is removed from human consumption. If cows returned equivalent nutrition in the form of meat, their feed would not be wasted. But the calorific energy provided by beef is only one-seventh of the calorific energy of the feed. This means that in the process of converting grain into beef, cows "waste" six-sevenths of the nutritional value of the planet's primary produce. The proportion is more favorable in poultry: an average chicken uses only two-thirds of the calorific value of the feed it consumes.

There is simply not enough grain to feed all the animals that would be needed to supply meat for the tables of the world's entire population. The giant herds of cattle and endless farms of poultry would require more grain than the total output of the agricultural lands — according to some calculations, about twice as much. Given the amount of land available for farming, and the known and presently used agricultural methods, doubling today's grain production would call for economically prohibitive investments.

This should make us pause — quite apart from the questionable viability of mass-producing beef and poultry for billions of avid consumers and the questionable ethics of doing so, indulging one segment of the world population while condemning another to malnutrition, if not downright starvation. A person who thinks globally eats what grows on the land, first and foremost in their own backyard or environment. Grain-based local and national food self-reliance could then allow the world's economically exploitable agricultural lands to feed the entire human population.

What goes for meat-eating also goes for smoking. The fact that smoking is dangerous to health can be read on every packet of cigarettes, but it is not generally known that the use of tobacco is unfair to millions of poor people in the world. The land on which most poor country farmers grow tobacco for export could be used for grain and vegetables to feed the local hungry. But, as long as there is a market, agribusinesses and farmers will plant tobacco instead of wheat, corn or soya, and there will be a market for tobacco as long as there is a demand in the global marketplace. And where demand is low multinational tobacco companies do their best to increase it.

Tobacco, together with other cash crops such as coffee and tea, commands a considerable portion of the world's fertile lands, yet no cash crop is a life necessity. Reducing the demand for red meat, coffee, and tobacco would mean a healthier life for the rich, and a chance for adequate nourishment for the poor.

Of course, abstaining from a heavy diet of meat, and overcoming dependence on tobacco or coffee would not automatically put more food on the tables of the world's poor. It would, however, make it possible for the world's productive lands to feed all people on the continents. If we go on as we do, this will not be possible. It takes over 12 acres to cover the average American's agriculture-related needs, while the needs of the average Indian are satisfied by one. For a population of six billion, up to four acres of land per person may be economically and technically feasible. But if we need to commit 12 acres of productive land for every human being, then two more planets the size of Earth would be required.

The use of automobiles is a further case in point. According to a World Bank estimate, by the year 2010 the population of motor vehicles will swell to one billion. This would double current levels of energy use, and could also double the level of smog precursors and greenhouse gases. Cars and trucks would choke the streets of big cities and the transportation arteries of entire economies. Yet this level of motor vehicle use is not a necessity. For goods transport, rails and rivers could be more effectively used, and for city dwellers public transport could be pressed into wide-scale service. The numbers of private vehicles could be reduced. Today's personal car is vastly overused. The ownership of expensive makes has become a matter of prestige. Driving responds to needs for personal aggrandizement, and gives vent to aggression above and beyond satisfying real needs for transportation.

Global thinking means thinking twice before taking a private car to town when public transport is available. It means taking pride in clean and well-kept subways, trams and buses, and traveling sociably in the company of others rather than in the air-conditioned and telephone and hi-fi equipped isolation of a personal car. For physically fit individuals short trips on a bicycle would make for a happier choice still: besides saving fuel, reducing traffic congestion, and cutting down on pollution, bikers benefit from an extra dose of fresh air and exercise.

Global thinking is not a personal matter, and not mere utopia. It can be practiced, and when practiced, it can have major and otherwise unattainable effects. This embraces impacts on land-use, on agricultural production and trade, on transportation systems, and on all things that affect the life and wellbeing of people in today's technological societies.

We know that the urban sprawl created by the widespread use of private automobiles is undesirable, that traffic jams are frustrating and counterproductive, and that the gasoline-powered internal combustion engine uses up finite resources, and contributes to air pollution and global warming. But though many people know this, the trend toward a growing reliance on gasoline-powered cars continues unchanged. It appears that as long as people are emotionally attached to such cars, and while a large number of jobs depend on their manufacture and use, industries will not make serious efforts to introduce alternatives, and states will not contemplate measures to curtail their circulation. Powerful lobbies intercede in favor of maintaining the profits of manufacturers, with their suppliers and distributors, service stations and repair shops, and the productivity of oil fields, refineries, and tankers. Alternative technologies are not pressed into use.

The situation would change if a critical mass of people began actively to demand cars propeled by renewable fuels, natural gas, liquid hydrogen, or electricity. Dealers would scramble to satisfy their customer's wishes; manufacturers would strive to satisfy the orders flowing from their dealers. Potential suppliers of the alternative technologies would find a new and high-growth market emerging before their eyes, ready to be exploited by imaginative entrepreneurs. Alcohol-based fuel and natural gas production would be stepped up, as would the production of efficient rechargeable batteries and, subsequently, of liquid hydrogen.

The development of the infrastructure required for the widespread use of these technologies would follow. Economists and trades unions would find that, though old jobs would need to be surrendered, new ones would be created. It would not be long before popular demand would catch the attention of politicians and legislators, and then a different set of policies and regulations would see the light of day. While considerable pockets of resistance would be likely to persist, a determined rise of demand could ultimately sweep them out of the way. As business people, politicians and economists well know, in a market economy there is nothing as powerful as popular demand.

Responsible choices

Global thinking becomes empowered when it finds expression in the spheres of acting and living. The rule of thumb is to act and live responsibly. Responsible acting and living means making considered choices in every sphere of existence:

• What consumer products do we purchase for our personal use — fancy items that use a great deal of energy, or simple and functional devices that do what we want to have done with a minimum of waste and fuss?

• What work or profession do we choose — something by which to amass the most money in the shortest time, or an activity that is meaningful in itself and beneficial to others?

• What technologies do we make use of in our enterprise — wasteful and polluting ones as long as they squeeze out a high rate of profit, or resource-efficient ones that respect nature and the community?

• How do we furnish our home — with synthetic ostentation, or for coziness, health, and sociability?

• What materials do we select for our home and personal use — non-biodegradable synthetics mass-produced in multinational chemical concerns, or natural fibers produced from plants in our own region?

• How do we clothe ourselves and our family — do we dress to be conspicuous, or for genuine self-expression? In ways that feed our ego, or in ways that preserve family and community values and our cultural heritage?

Our responsibilities go deeper than we may think. In today's world all individuals, no matter where they live and what they do, have multiple roles in society and there are responsibilities attaching to each. We are at the same time private persons; citizens of our country; collaborators in a business; actors in an economy; members of the human community; and persons endowed with a unique mind and consciousness.[2]

In order to live up to these responsibilities, we have to respect a small set of precepts:

• To be careful not to act and consume in ways that would prevent the options of others to act and consume in a similar way — not just out of a cool calculation of resource availability and ecological carrying capacity, but because of our feeling of solidarity with our community, nation and culture, and the global community of peoples, nations and cultures.

• To seek simple and natural foods, materials and lifestyles, to rejoice in nature, to reject uncleanliness, waste, and pollution.

• To avoid ostentation in personal appearance, at home and in workplaces, expressing instead genuine human and cultural values.

• To derive satisfaction from making thoughtful and moral choices in all facets of existence — choices that enhance the chances of life and development for other people, whether they live in our immediate environment or in more distant places.

The rule of thumb for responsible living is encapsulated in the dictum: "Live in a way that others can live as well." This goes beyond the familiar *laissez-faire* tenet "live and let live." An up-to-date concept is required: in an interdependent and increasingly crowded planet, letting people live in any way they may wish is not a desirable option. The rich and the powerful would consume a disproportionate share of the planet's resources, and this would prevent access to vital resources for many others. The *laissez-faire* philosophy needs to be hedged with timely cautions. It is more responsible to make sure that all people live in a way that all others can also live.

This rule is not new. It is akin to philosopher Emmanuel Kant's categorical imperative: "Act so that your action can become a universal maxim." In today's context it tells us that we should live and act in a way that could be replicated in principle by all people without depressing the humanly relevant carrying capacity of the planet.

Living in a "universalizable" way is not necessarily a sacrifice. It does not mean being self-denying: one can continue to strive for excellence and beauty, personal growth and enjoyment, even for comfort and luxury. But in a responsible lifestyle the pleasures and achievements of life are defined in terms of the quality of enjoyment and level of satisfaction they provide, rather than concern with the amount of money they cost, or the quantity of materials and energy that goes into them. Material standards of living and quality of life are distinct measures, and beyond a certain point they pull in opposite directions. Affluence in monetary and material terms tends to depress the quality of life; competition, stress, and egoistic concerns interfere with the enjoyment of life's simpler and more genuine pleasures.

A switch from lifestyles oriented toward maximum consumption and maximum purchasing power, toward ways of life hallmarked by a search for responsibly achievable personal and community values, presupposes a fundamental shift in mentality. Most people still value goods and services in direct proportion to their price and material and energy content; the privileged strata still live in a way that the less privileged cannot duplicate. The planet has neither the resources nor the carrying capacity for all people to drive private cars, live in separate homes, eat a meat diet, and use the myriad appliances that go with the current lifestyle of the affluent.

Changes are also called for on the part of the less privileged: they, in turn, must not aspire to the lifestyles that they normally associate with wealth and privilege. It would not be enough for well-to-do Americans, Europeans, and Japanese to reduce harmful industrial, residential, and transport emissions and cut down on gross energy consumption if the Chinese and the rest of the poor countries were to continue to burn coal for electricity and wood for cooking, implement classical industrial-age economic policies, and acquire Western driving and consumer habits. Acting in accordance with the ground rule "live in a way that others can live as well" calls for responsibility by all people, not only the privileged, and not only the poor.

CHAPTER 4

CREATING A NEW ENTERPRISE CULTURE

Responsible and up-to-date thinking and acting by individuals is one of the imperatives of our times; another is the behavior of entire groups and institutions. Among these, the actions and strategies of business corporations are particularly important: global enterprises wield unprecedented power and influence. Fifty of the world's largest businesses have sales that exceed the GNP of over 100 national states. Though the top 500 of the world's industrial corporations employ only 0.05 per cent of the world's population, they control 70 per cent of world trade, and 25 per cent of the world's economic output.

Business corporations do not obey rules imposed by outside sources unless they are backed by legal and economic sanctions — and then they tend to resist them as undue restrictions on the operations of the free market. Instead, executives adopt their own codes and rules for guiding corporate behavior. These codes and rules are part of the culture of modern corporations.

In the past, corporate culture recognized few restrictions on the twin goals of seeking profit and growth for the greater good of the stockholders. But recently a number of additional considerations have emerged. In the culture of leading corporations short-term profit-seeking has come to be modulated by concerns with enduring profitability, and unqualified growth-seeking has been replaced with a search for a sustainable share in a variety of markets. Managers are placing increasing emphasis on the philosophy, identity, and role of their enterprise, and the role and ethics of its leadership. Notwithstanding the scepticism of some analysts and investors regarding visionary strategies and values-based organizations, and a hard core of resistance to abandoning the "shareholder value is all there is" philosophy, a major shift is under way in the culture of leading corporations.

There are good reasons for the shift in corporate culture: the culture of the classical industrial-age enterprise is now obsolete. Its centerpiece was profit and growth achieved on the premise that the business of business is simply business, that good products and services will sell themselves, and if not, marketing will create demand for them. If a company comes up with saleable products, it will maximize its profits and growth, and fulfil all reasonable demands on its behavior.

In the closing years of this century this simplistic premise no longer guarantees either profit or growth. An executive who adopts it is like a pilot who concentrates all his skills on flying his airplane but pays scant attention to the airspace in which he is flying. Today's captains need to be concerned with more than the functioning of their aircraft: they must also set a course taking account of climatic conditions, current position and projected destination, and traffic on the network of routes criss-crossing the globe. That traffic is diversified and complex. Today's business environment includes, in addition to customers, suppliers, distributors, R&D partners, technology sub-contractors, government departments and ministries, and numerous cooperative and competitive enterprises, also the social, ecological, and cultural trends and movements that unfold at the various locations of operation.

Belief in the adequacy of inward-looking efficiency was one pillar of classical industrial-age enterprise culture; belief in the effectiveness of a hierarchical form of organization was another. For most of the 20th century, operating on the basis of a company hierarchy produced acceptable profit and growth. Following the prescriptions of Frederick Taylor's "scientific management", top management could command a company without being influenced by, or even much concerned with, its lower echelons. Motivation for task-fulfillment was created by material incentives bolstered by threats; individual creativity and initiative were dismissed as unnecessary nuisance. The distribution of tasks was established at headquarters and the company's functions were divided into individual work components. Planning was based on a belief in control and predictability, effects were traced to causes, and causes were quantitatively analyzed. Company operations based on cause-effect chains were given value independent of time and place: as in a machine, it was held that the same input would always produce the same output.

This was the philosophy of the leading companies of the early and mid-20th century, the model for success at General Motors and Standard Oil, and most of the other giants of the Fortune 500 group. The economic growth-environment of the post-war period did not provide grounds to question the classical management culture. Almost anything an enterprising manager would try had a knack of succeeding; he could also engage in personal bravado. Technological progress seemed assured, and expanding markets seemed to distribute the benefits of growth.

The post-war economy welcomed all entrepreneurs; they could grow as the economy did. Long-term costs were safely hidden in the long term. Businessmen were fond of quoting Keynes: "In the long term we shall all be dead." Indeed, if things were getting better and better, why bother to look further than one's nose? There was no need to worry whether or not there would be progress, it was enough to guess what shape it would take, and how one could best benefit from it.

In the 1970s the situation changed. The curves of economic indicators flattened, extrapolations of continued linear growth did not come true. Social alienation and anomie rose, and technology produced unexpected side-effects: scares and catastrophes at Three Mile Island, Bhopal, and Chernobyl, the ozone hole over the Antarctic, recurrent instances of acid rain and oil spill, and worsening environmental pollution in cities and on land. Belief in reliable technologically driven progress was shaken. Intellectuals and youth groups found it necessary, and some segments of society fashionable, to espouse the view that technological advance is dangerous and should be halted. Environmental effects and social value-change began to enter as factors in equations of corporate success, and leading managers, together with consultants and management theorists, began to re-examine their operative assumptions.

In the 1980s further changes occurred in the business world. New technologies came on line, markets became integrated and internationalized, product cycles became shorter and product lines diversified, and clients and consumers demanded shorter delivery times and higher quality. At the same time, environmental concerns moved from the fringes of society into the marketplace. Consumers proved willing to pay a premium for products they deemed environmentally friendly, and were known to boycott companies that remained part of the smokestack complex.

Competition moved into the global arena, and inward-looking hierarchically organized enterprises proved unable to compete. The centralization of information and its slow one-way penetration to lower echelons produced fatal mistakes, if not terminal rigidity. The companies that survived did so by transforming themselves into socially and environmentally responsive decision-making and operational structures — often in the nick of time.

In the 1990s not only information, but also people, emerged as a key resource of any enterprise; and teamwork proved to be the best way to tap it. Hierarchies flattened as decision-making became team-based and distributed. Cost-cutting through reductions at the workplace, together with growth in the number of interfaces among more intensely employed people in interlinked departments and business units, made organizational structures flat as well as highly mobile. Fusions, alliances, and strategic partnerships created mobility also in the wider industry environment; boundaries between a company and its economic, social, and ecological environment became increasingly hazy. Even core activities came to be subcontracted — work relations with other firms became almost as commonplace as company-based operations. Reliance on distributors and suppliers, and linkage to local communities and ecologies, emerged as standard parameters of corporate functioning; cooperation emerged as a complement to competition.

Today's leading players bear little resemblance to the classical industrial-age corporations, and with good reason. Concentration on the internal operations of the company is not enough; there is a need for broad vision and keen responsiveness to social and environmental trends and developments. Hierarchical structures are increasingly inefficient — they have to be replaced by lean organizational modalities and reliance on partner- and staff-consultation based on two-way flows of information and communication. Managers need to respond to an increasing range of critical issues. They need to cope with unpredictable economic conditions, develop sufficient flexibility for using new technologies as they come on line, enable their companies to enter new fields of activity and leave old ones, and keep track of the growing diversity of their partners and competitors.

The wages of the cutting edge

In the early 1970s, when the first oil crisis shook world industry with increased energy costs affecting pricing, and high inflation undermining consumer confidence, it was widely believed that being at the cutting edge meant increasing productivity. Higher productivity allowed companies to produce more without increasing their raw material, capital, and labor inputs, meaning they could pass on savings on production costs to the customers. Owing to a further rise in energy costs, in the late 1970s businesses had to renew their fight to maintain their market share, and the answer, managers held, lay in higher quality. Quality control circles and total quality management led to more favorable cost-structures and increased customer loyalty.

In the increasingly competitive environment of the 1980s staying at the cutting edge required yet another factor, and managers espoused the concept of "just-in-time" as the answer. Just-in-time deliveries reduced delay times, cut stocking costs, and permitted increases in overall production efficiency. Then, in the 1990s, the key factor of ongoing competitivity came to be viewed as service. Up to three-quarters of the value added by industry consists today of production-related services, and an entire industry has grown up to satisfy the need. Japanese companies outsource some 16 per cent of all services to third-party professionals, and this proportion, though initially lower in Europe and America, is growing throughout the industrialized world.

As we enter the third millennium productivity, quality, just-in-time, and service-orientation remain principal requisites of staying with the cutting edge, but they are not the only ones. The additional factor is *responsibility*. Any company's responsibility extends beyond concern with the production, use, servicing, and disposal of the products it manufactures, and the utility of the legal, financial, health, or other services it provides. It encompasses all issues that impact on the life and wellbeing of its stakeholders, whether they are employees, shareholders, clients, customers, or just members of the communities where it operates. Their welfare — and hence their satisfaction, and ability to buy company products and pay for company services — is directly or indirectly bound up with the company's ethics and sense of responsibility.

Responsibility for the stakeholders must be more than skin-deep. PR claims and cosmetic solutions are not sufficient as customers are getting smarter, better informed about product quality, price, availability, and service, and more selective about the companies they wish to patronize and do business with. Recent surveys in Europe show that less than 10 per cent of the public believes claims of environmental and social responsibility by companies unless they are backed by tangible evidence. Surveys in the United States indicate that over 40 per cent of consumers say that, when price and quality are comparable, their choice is influenced by the issues they believe are genuinely important to the companies. Market analyses in Europe and Japan testify that high standards and commitment to social and environmental issues are key factors of competition in an environment where market success means providing higher perceived value at lower price. No longer simply an idealistic "soft" factor, responsibility for stakeholders has become a "hard" dimension of the enterprise culture.

Stakeholder satisfaction in terms of perceived value means not only a zero-defect production process with minimal cost, efficient marketing, and a full range of services, but also incorporates a full commitment of responsibility to all the people with whom the company does business.

Social and environmental responsibility pays off: in client and consumer satisfaction, stockholder approval, and a healthier and better educated public with higher purchasing power. This in itself is not new: as research by Collins and Porns on the habits of visionary companies has shown, a common feature of the most successful companies in the United States for the past 100 years has been a culture that was entirely value-driven, with a focus on an enduring purpose that had little to do with immediate profit. These factors continue to pay off today, for example, for Mary Kay Cosmetics, Walmart, and Ikea in empowering the underdog; Ben & Jerry's and The Body Shop in social and environmental activism; and Merck, Honda, Sony, and 3M in efforts to produce responsible technological innovations.

When public responsibility as a goal is embraced by managers, it pays off for the managers themselves. The law profession has justice as its lofty goal; the medical profession health. But managers lack a clearly defined ideal, other than making money for their company and thereby creating wealth for society. This goal, though valid in itself, tends to blur into personal and corporate greed and lose legitimacy. And its power to motivate people is not as great as generally assumed. Large numbers of people will not ultimately give their all for protracted periods of time for an abstraction called a corporation, or an idea called profit. People can only give to people; they can give to their co-workers if they believe that they are engaged together in an enterprise of some importance; they can give to society, which is another way of saying that they can give to their children. They can give if they believe that their work is in some way integrated into a whole life. Embracing responsibility for all stakeholders furnish a valid and effective goal. It provides new motivation for managers, and helps restore society's faith in their profession.

Young people still aspire to power and fame, but look for it less and less in the corporate ranks. As reported in the Financial Times of 6th June 1997, in a survey of 140 MBA students at the London Business School, only six students were found who aspired to management positions in established corporations — the others hoped to derive professional satisfaction by broadening and deepening their personal portfolio of skills and contributing to society in more meaningful ways.

Adopting responsibility for the stakeholders means creating a company culture where a sense of total responsibility complements the striving for total quality. Such a culture is beneficial for both managers and companies, but achieving it may involve some level of corporate sacrifice. The latter could be a problem: in cases where the pay-offs are in the more distant future, executives may be discouraged from pursuing the strategies of transformation. Feasible ways must be found to bridge the gap between initial investment and expected pay-off. Companies must grow toward stakeholder responsibility without losing market share, or disappointing stockholders, and while continuing to allow competitors and free riders to exploit interim problems and sacrifices for their own narrow interests.

This requirement is not likely to be met by individual companies by themselves, regardless of how large and powerful they may be. Recent restructuring — or re-engineering or re-design — efforts, though driven by highly motivated executives and advised by first rate consultancy firms, have proven to be both expensive and frustrating. The New Leaders reported that, while US corporations spent over 200 billion US dollars in 1993 on attempting to change, retrain, or in some way revise their organizations, fewer than 20 per cent of the managers authorizing the layouts were pleased with the outcomes — a proportion that dropped to 16 per cent in a poll of executives carried out by Arthur D. Little. And the May-June 1997 issue of the Journal of Business Strategy reported that in Gemini Consulting's survey of 782 corporations only 47 per cent of the executives claimed to have succeeded in generating a growth of revenue; 37 per cent had managed to raise market share, and merely 8 per cent ranked change in the organizational structure among their top three priorities.

A thoroughgoing transformation capable of enabling a company to achieve stakeholder responsibility is likely to call for joint efforts. There are numerous precedents for this: partners and competitors in the information and communication, electronics, airline, automobile, pharmaceutical, and other sectors often join forces for purposes of R&D, production, or marketing. There is no reason why market leaders could not also forge partnerships in the interest of evolving a stakeholder responsibility culture in their own branch of industry.

Total Responsibility Management (TRM) needs to be embraced to complement Total Quality Management (TQM). To add TRM to TQM the creation of Total Responsibility Councils (TRCs) may be an efficient strategy. The Councils could design industry-wide codes of conduct of stakeholder responsibility with application to all players, including smaller and possibly less ethical competitors. Given the participation of a critical mass of market leaders and the advice of an independent group of advisors, TRCs could command adequate insight to oversee the code's provisions, and sufficient muscle to enforce compliance with them.[3]

The growing number of seminars on the role and responsibility of corporate management in America, Europe, and Japan, and the spate of best-selling management books on the social and environmental responsibility of corporations, indicate that forward-looking leaders in the business community are ready to embrace total stakeholder responsibility. This is with good reason: they know that in a globally outreaching and interacting socio-economic and ecological system only responsible companies can lead — or even survive.

CHAPTER 5

LIFTING THE SIGHTS
OF GOVERNMENT

Traditionally, responsibility for the people was the concern of the political leadership. Such responsibility is now shared by global corporations, but it is not abrogated by them: governments remain responsible for caring for the welfare of their people, hand in hand with the business community.

For governments to live up to their share of the responsibility, they must lift their sights beyond the borders of the states they govern. With few exceptions, this has not yet happened. Similarly to the inward-looking disposition of classical managers, the perceptions of national politicians remain strongly centered on the interests of their own constituencies. This in itself is neither wrong nor surprising: the interests of their constituencies need to be represented, and it is right that they should be represented by the institutions that were created for that very purpose. However, the interests of today's national constituencies can no more be represented by inward-looking strategies than the interests of today's business enterprises. Just as the vision of managers needs to expand from the functions of their company to its relationships and role in the local and global environment, so the sights of national politicians need to rise from the level of their own nation-states to the whole of the interconnected and interdependent world community.

Lifting the sights of government is both urgent and imperative. The way most democracies work, national leaders, if they are to stay in power, need to confine their attention to the few problems that occupy the public's attention; they cannot afford to pay much attention to a host of issues that may be just as, or even more, important. Action on complex and controversial problems calls for time-consuming public and legislative debate, and carries political risks that politicians do not embrace unless they have strong motivation to do so. It is easier and more politically expedient to ignore people who raise issues that do not have the attention of the media and the public — or the backing of influential lobbies and pressure groups. In consequence governmental action tends to be narrowly focused and neglectful of many of the issues that shape the contemporary world.

The political process itself selects against commitment to basic and long-term issues. Ballots carry the names of individuals who for the most part have a taste for power and a high level of competitiveness. Those who prefer cooperation to competition, knowledge to power, and are concerned with long-term issues seldom present themselves to election. As economist Kenneth Boulding's "dismal theorem" states, most of the skills that lead to the rise of political power make those who possess the skills unfit to exercise the power.

Nevertheless, political figures often show a significant level of commitment to the public good and a genuine wish to serve it. Yet even when their intentions are genuine and honorable, their actions tend to be less than effective. If they become aware of issues that are of fundamental importance but not (or not yet) in the public eye, they can fund studies, make reports, and hold conferences. But, unless they receive public approbation, they cannot act. As Vice President Al Gore observed in Earth in the Balance: "Ironically, at this stage, the maximum that is politically feasible still falls short of the minimum that is truly effective."

Effectiveness is also reduced by the fact that in some respects contemporary nation-states are too big to cope with some pertinent issues, and in others they are too small to implement desirable and workable solutions. Decisions that touch people's lives, whether through education, employment, law-and-order, or civil liberties, require decision-making that is closer to the grass-roots than the majority of today's national governments. On the other hand decision-making in the economic sphere requires a sphere of competence that is larger than the majority of contemporary nation-states — economies of scale are essential with regard to the exploitation and use of natural resources, as well as for the efficient employment of labor and the effective marketing of products and services. This holds true for territorial and ecological security as well. National armies can no more ensure the inviolability of a country's borders than national regulations can safeguard the integrity of its natural environment.

Beyond the myth of the nation-state

Lifting the sights of national governments above the borders of their country, and focusing them on economic, social, and cultural regions outside it, is an urgent necessity. Fortunately, this is not a utopian proposition. Limited sights are due to the dominance of the myth of the sovereign nation-state, and not to factors rooted in the nature of society or the nature of people.

The formally constituted nation-state is a historical phenomenon: in its legally constituted form it appeared on the world scene only at the Peace of Westphalia in 1648. In the 17th and 18th centuries nation-states spread throughout Europe, and in the 20th century the wave of decolonization following World War Two extended them to all parts of the world. Leaders of the decolonized countries objected to almost everything they inherited from their former colonial masters but never contested the principle of national sovereignty. As a result, the world community now consists of nearly 200 nation-states, including economic giants such as the United States, population giants such as China and India, and a plethora of small and poor states such as Guyana, Benin, and the Seychelles.

Decision-making in a world dominated by nation-states is cumbersome, as the experience of the United Nations testifies. But the reform of today's national sovereignty-based system is feasible. There are no factors in the psychology of individuals that would limit the expansion of personal loyalty above, or its focusing below, the level of a national state. No individual is obliged by his or her emotional make-up to swear exclusive allegiance to one flag only, in the conviction that it symbolizes "my country, right or wrong." People can be loyal to several segments of society without being disloyal to any. They can be loyal to their community without giving up loyalty to their province, state, or region. They can be loyal to their region and also feel at one with an entire culture, and with the human family as a whole. As Europeans are English,

Germans, French, Spanish, and Italians as well as Europeans, and as Americans are New Englanders, Texans, Southerners, and Pacific Northwesterners as well as Americans, so people in all parts of the world possess multiple identities, and can develop the multiple allegiances that go with them.

Decentralizing the powers of national governments is urgent and important with regard to conditions that impact on the education, employment, social security, social and economic justice, and local resource use of people in grass-roots communities and in ethnic and minority groups. In turn, decentralization in the upward direction is urgent in order to cope with two of the most pressing issues of our times: peace and security, and ecological sustainability.

That national security would call for a powerful national defense force is as much of a myth as unconditional national sovereignty. When national security is reexamined in the context of the emerging world system, it becomes evident that in many cases it can be more reliably ensured by regional defense pacts backed up by joint defense forces, rather than by national armies commanded by a central government. In a number of European countries the logic of shifting security from the national to the regional level has already dawned on the public. People in Scandinavia, the Benelux region, and on the rim of the Mediterranean, show themselves open to the idea of joint defense forces. Even in conservative Switzerland, the population proved flexible on this score. In November 1989, when the socialists collected sufficient signatures to hold a referendum on whether to abolish the Swiss army, over 30 per cent of the people voted for doing so. This went counter to popular expectations which, in view of the high esteem in which the Swiss people have traditionally held their army, estimated that no more than 5-6 per cent of the population would back such a drastic step.

Many medium and small European countries are ready to acknowledge that it is pointless for them to maintain an expensive army apparatus when they could assure good internal and external security with much smaller expenditures — the former through a well-equipped police force or national guard, and the latter through a regional peacekeeping force. But the great majority of contemporary states are not ready to entrust their national defense to collective peacekeeping. The sovereignty myth is compelling, even if joint peacekeeping by UN forces proved its mettle in some of the world's worst trouble spots, and notwithstanding the promise that joint peacekeeping would free the participating economies from the burden of maintaining costly armies and enable their government to use the liberated human and financial resources for productive ends.

The other area where lifting the sights of government to the global level is urgent and important is the environment. The objectives of a global system of environmental monitoring and action have been extensively discussed and are relatively well known. They focus on the regulation of the mining and use of natural resources; on the safeguarding of the balances and regenerative cycles of nature; and on the creation of emergency capacities for dealing with environmental disasters and catastrophes. Implementing these objectives is in every country's vital interest. Every economy needs an assured supply of natural resources and every population needs a healthy environment.

Yet, despite "Agenda 21" and other plans and conventions, cooperation in the environmental domain remains underfinanced and largely on the level of rhetoric. Only half a dozen countries have levied environmental taxes to discourage the unsustainable use of natural resources and energy, while many governments continue to subsidize the clear-cutting of forests, strip mining, and inefficient uses of water. In Europe, some 63 per cent of direct subsidy to the energy industry goes to fossil fuels and 28 per cent to the nuclear industry; in the US, these proportions are 58 and 30 per cent. With the exception of the ozone-destroying CFC reduction convention (encouraged by the availability of economically viable alternatives), governments are not prepared to bind themselves to specific environmental goals and targets: they consider them an infringement on their national sovereignty.

While the debates go on, and statements of principle are negotiated, few of them are fully ratified and even fewer translated into practice. As a result the stocks of nonrenewable resources continue to be depleted, regenerative capacities for a number of renewable resources are further impaired, and the overall livability of the environment is depressed. The global emission of carbon from fossil fuels is soaring, expected to exceed 1990 levels by 17 per cent at the turn of the millennium, and 49 percent by the year 2010. Forests are disappearing: North and Central America have less than a century of forests remaining, the Caribbean less than 50 years, the Philippines 30 years, Afghanistan 16 years, and Lebanon 15 years. A third of the planet's total land surface is threatened with desertification; a hundred or more species are lost each day, and the atmosphere is heating up, producing unstable weather patterns and threatening a rise in world sea levels. Razali Ismail, the Secretary General of the second "Earth Summit" called to review progress since Rio, pointed out that we face a major recession, one that is not economic, but of the spirit. "We continue", he said, "to consume resources, pollute, and entrench poverty as though we are the last generation on Earth."

The myth of sovereignty is blocking progress regarding matters that are of concern to all the world's peoples. The attention of national governments is centered on short-term and narrowly focused issues, backed by powerful lobbies and local constituencies. This state of affairs is neither desirable nor sustainable. In order truly to represent their people's interests, governments must expand their sights. They need selectively to transfer powers of decision-making above as well as below the national borders. In the upward direction they need to transfer powers in selected domains to jointly constituted regional organizations or global bodies. And in the downward direction they need to transfer some of the powers vested in national institutions to smaller-scale, social, economic and cultural regions as well as to grass-roots and ethnic and minority groups.

In our complex and interdependent world, effectiveness and efficiency come about through widely networked cooperative structures. This holds just as true in the world of politics as in the world of business.

CHAPTER 6

ADOPTING A CODE FOR ENVIRONMENTAL MORALITY

In various spheres of human affairs, the dawn of the 21st century marks a major decision point. We could move toward a system of social, economic, and political organization capable of ensuring an adequate level of sustainability for our life-supporting environment, but we could also create conditions that are distinctly disadvantageous for human life and wellbeing. We could create a tenable global civilization, or find ourselves on a path of growing ecological crises and catastrophes. The choice is still open.

The questions surrounding this choice do have a pragmatic dimension: our own future is at stake. But the answers are far from evident: actions that serve our own interests may be indifferent, or disastrous, for others around us. The "parable of the common" suggested by ecologist Garret Hardin helps to frame the issue.

Take a common, said Hardin, where ten shepherds each have ten sheep grazing. Suppose that one hundred sheep is the limit of the capacity of the common to regenerate its vegetation and enable it to function as grazing land for sheep. The shepherds are all ambitious businessmen: they wish to maximize their profits. Each shepherd reasons that if he adds one more sheep to his flock, he will add one-tenth to his profits, but only one-hundredth to the load on the common. This sounds reasonable. But it is not: if every shepherd decided to act on it, the capacity of the common would be drastically exceeded — the vegetation cover would soon vanish. This would not serve any shepherd's true interest.

The need for moral codes

Ensuring the viability of the environment within which we live is essential for all of us. But how do we achieve it when tooth-and-claw competition and short-sighted self-interest are still dominant? Governments need to lift their sights to the interdependence of states and communities with each other and with nature; business leaders need to evolve a corporate culture of total responsibility for their stakeholders. But mainstream society also needs to muster its collective will and commitment. All people need to embrace compelling norms for responsible behavior, with authoritative codes regarding the limits of human impact on the environment.

Moral codes are informal guideposts and not legislated laws, so they are only enforceable by the approbation or disapprobation of society. This, however, can be highly effective. By stating the publicly accepted norms of socially desirable behavior, moral codes can play a major role in orienting people's goals and aspirations.

Traditionally, the world's great religions have set the codes of public morality — the Ten Commandments of Jews and Christians, the provisions for the faithful in Islam, and the Rules of Right Livelihood of the Buddhists. Today, the advance of science has reduced the power of religious doctrine-based codes for moral behavior. However, even though science displaced religion as a source of authority, scientists have not come up with an ethics that could ground authoritative moral codes. There have been some attempts. Saint-Simon in the late 1700s, Auguste Compte in the early 1800s, and Emile Durkheim in the late 1800s and early 1900s were at pains to develop "positive" — scientific observation- and experiment-based — codes for moral behavior. However, the endeavor as a whole was so opposed to the underlying ideology of modern science — its commitment to value neutrality and bare objectivity — that it was not taken up by the mainstream of 20th-century science communities.

Now, as we enter the third millennium, the need for an ethic that suggests acceptable codes for moral behavior is becoming more widely recognized. The Parliament of the World's Religions, convening in 1993 in Chicago, called for a global ethic based on four time-honored guidelines for human behavior: a culture of non-violence and respect for life; a just economic order; a culture of tolerance and a life of truthfulness; and a culture of equal rights and partnership between men and women. This, the representatives of the world's religions noted, is a "minimal ethic that is absolutely necessary for human survival." The Union of Concerned Scientists was of the same opinion. "A new ethic is required," claimed a statement signed on the 18th November 1993, by 1,670 scientists from 70 countries, including 102 Nobel Laureates. "This ethic must motivate a great movement, convincing reluctant leaders, and reluctant governments, and reluctant peoples themselves to effect the needed changes."

The ethic that the scientists had in mind was primarily environmental. They spoke of our "new responsibility" for caring for the Earth. They issued a warning that "a great change in our stewardship of the Earth and the life on it is required if vast human misery is to be avoided and our global home on this planet is not to be irretrievably mutilated... We must recognize the Earth's limited capacity to provide for us... We must no longer allow it to be ravaged." The ravage is serious: "Our massive tampering with the world's interdependent web of life — coupled with the environmental damage which is inflicted by deforestation, species loss, and climate change — could trigger widespread adverse effects, including unpredictable collapses of critical biological systems whose interactions and dynamics we only imperfectly understand. Human beings and the natural world are on a collision course... that may so alter the living world that it will be unable to sustain life in the manner that we know."

Uncertainty over the extent of the effects, the scientists added, cannot excuse complacency or delay in facing the threats. Yet complacency and delay abound: political and business leaders act on the maxim that if a policy or strategy is not proven to be bad, there is no need to touch it. For the most part they are reluctant to make significant investments and initiate meaningful programs to safeguard our ability to live on this increasingly ravaged planet. Further warnings and declarations will not suffice by themselves: there must also be behavioral codes that a critical mass of people can accept — and respect.

The nature of a sound environmental code

There is an emerging consensus as to the content of an effective and desirable moral code for the environment: such a code must motivate behavior capable of creating conditions of long-term *sustainability*. The term "sustainability" stems from forestry, where it was used to refer to a harvest of trees whch was sufficient to cover current needs without impairing the productivity of the forest for future tree generations. In the 1960s environmentalists picked it up; and in 1987 the UN's Brundtland's Commission made it into a pillar of international negotiations. At the 1992 Global Summit of Rio de Janeiro it emerged as the key concept.

Used officially, sustainability refers to several "maintainabilities": the maintainability of a single natural resource (such as trees); the maintainability of the regenerative capacity of an entire resource-system (such as harvests, in view of adequate biodiversity); as well as the overall maintainability of the relationship between human welfare — including that of future generations — social structure, and natural process. In its popular use the concept is simpler: it hallmarks aspirations and behaviors that do not destroy the natural processes on which life essentially depends.

The matter is by no means simple, however. If behavior is to contribute to the sustainability of the environment, the codes that sanction it must take into account that ecological conditions change over time. Natural ecologies undergo structural and functional changes, some piecemeal and linear, others more radical and nonlinear. So behavior must be adapted not only to the current state of the environment, but also to its foreseeable evolution. An effective moral code must take evolutionary change into account. It must sanction behavior that not only maintains current ecological processes, but allows or promotes their unfolding.

Even such a code falls short of the mark, however. Developmental processes in nature are constantly accelerating, and a continued acceleration could spell doom for the species that cannot keep up with it. This unfortunate lemma may apply to the human species as well.

Evolutionary acceleration in nature is remarkably constant. Not only have more and more species emerged in the course of evolutionary time, but the rate of their evolution has also been speeding up. Over half the time in biological evolution was taken up with the advance from the stage of the non-nucleated prokaryotic cells to that of the nucleated eukaryotes; thereafter it took evolution only half that span of time to reach the level of fish. Time intervals between the major evolutionary steps have continued to shorten. The Miocene epoch was about 25 million years ago, while the Lower Pleistocene or the Quaternary began 1.6 million years ago, the Middle Pleistocene 750,000 years ago, and the Upper

Pleistocene was only 125,000 years before our time. Hominid creatures appeared during the Holocene (or Recent) epoch, though our lineage may have diverged from other hominoid species long before then.

Thereafter human evolution shifted from the genetic to the sociocultural mode and its rate moved up by another order of magnitude. Organized societies with *rites de passage*, writing, and other sociocultural practices appeared about 20,000 years ago; the first varieties of plants and animals were domesticated eight to ten thousand years before our time; and the great empires of the Middle and Far East appeared a few thousand years later. At the dawn of the modern age technology became the principal driver of evolution in the human realm. Balances in the biosphere were disturbed by interventions that destroyed some species and created developmental space for others.

Driven by newly discovered energy sources, first steam and then coal, oil, and natural gas, and impelled by technologies for processing, storing and transmitting information, human interventions in nature intensified. Some of their consequences proved unforeseen and undesirable, and some unpredictable. This, however, cannot be an excuse for inaction. If current interventions were to intensify further, humanity would be condemned to join the ranks of the over 99 per cent of multicellular species that have become extinct since the great evolutionary burst of the Cambrian epoch 600 million years ago. Our place would be taken by species that are better adapted than us to the conditions our interventions bring about: low fertility soils, high sea levels, warm climates, a thin ozone layer, and strong radiations.

Upon due reflection we must come to the conclusion that an effective environmental code must not only allow or promote the evolutionary processes that hold sway in nature and society; it must also motivate the behavior to maintain these processes within the bounds of conditions favorable to human life and wellbeing. The biological basis of human life — use of soil, water, air, and habitable space, even the physiology of our bodies — is adapted to conditions that have reigned on Earth for several thousand years. Brusque changes in these conditions have an overwhelming probability of reducing our ability to survive. Under certain conditions, a slowing down of evolutionary change is desirable.

Individual and social behavior needs to be committed to the maintenance of favorable conditions in the biosphere. The relevant maxim is not "sustain the current state of nature's basic life-support systems," and not even "promote the further evolution of nature's life-support systems." The indicated principle is to "*maintain an ongoing dynamic equilibrium between resources required to sustain essential human needs and reasonable demands, and the planet's self-regenerating life-support systems.*"

Adopting this code is urgent. In the absence of the corresponding actions nature's life-support systems could evolve along pathways which could turn out to be distinctly inhospitable to human communities. Agricultural lands could erode; weather patterns could turn hostile; water tables could sink and ocean levels rise; lethal radiations could penetrate the atmosphere; and microorganisms which are fundamentally incompatible with the human organism could proliferate. A variety of local eco-catastrophes could occur. On the other hand, adoption of this code could motivate individual and collective behavior aimed at true sustainability: the creation of an enduring dynamic equilibrium between the requirements of individual, social, and economic development, and the regenerative capacities of the biosphere's systems of water, air, energy, and land.

CHAPTER 7

SHIFTING TO A CULTURE OF INTEREXISTENCE

Culture is a powerful factor in human affairs: it enters into all we see and feel. There is no "immaculate perception" — everything we perceive comes to us colored by expectations and prejudices. These are largely set by our culture: we see the world through culturally tinted spectacles. The great majority of people use these spectacles without knowing that they do, and their cultural bias is all the more powerful for being invisible. What people do is strongly dependent on what they believe, and what they believe depends in part on the culturally colored vision they have of themselves and the world.

Although they are exposed to pressures toward uniformity and leveling, living cultures still differ one from another in values, outlooks, and visions of man and cosmos. Their diversity merits deeper acquaintance, for it shapes the attitudes and behaviors of the people of each culture. More than that: through the impact of each culture on all other cultures, it shapes relations in our entire multicultural world — and thus the future of this world.

A palette of cultural diversity

In the course of history the cultures of humankind evolved and elaborated their visions. At the dawn of history the world was seen atavistically: not only humans, but also animals and plants had souls; all of nature was alive. A watering hole in the savannah inspired awe for the spirits and forces of nature and for the souls of the dead; a deer appearing in the midst of human settlements was the spirit of an ancestor drawn back to his kinsfolk; thunder was a sign from a primordial Mother or an omnipotent Father... Throughout recorded history, traditional cultures overlaid sensory perceptions with unseen beings in symbolic hierarchies.

The classical cultures of Greece replaced worldviews based on myth with conceptions derived from reasoning, though these conceptions were seldom tested with experiments and observations. But since biblical times in the West, and since earlier millennia in the East, people's worldviews were dominated by the precepts and images of their religions and spiritual beliefs. This influence waned only in the 16th and 17th centuries, when experimental science arose in Europe. In the last three centuries scientific-technological culture overlaid, though it did not entirely replace, the mythical and religious worldviews of the Middle Ages.

In the 20th century Western scientific-technological culture has spread to the far corners of the world. Non-Western cultures now face the dilemma whether to open up to this culture, or close off and continue to follow their traditional ways of living, working, and worshipping.

Western culture is individualistic and person-centered. It holds sacrosanct the personal values of life, liberty, and the pursuit of happiness. Nature, and indeed the rest of creation, exist primarily for the benefit of enterprising individuals. Western culture is also pragmatic: it dismisses almost everything that cannot be seen and grasped — whatever is not "manifest" to hand and eye. The exception is the Judeo-Christian belief system, with its transcendent God, panoply of saints and otherworldly beliefs, including belief in an immortal soul. As to the spirits and other unseen and unseeable entities held in awe by traditional cultures, the science-minded face of Western culture dismisses them as mere prejudice, though the populace at large often holds contrary beliefs — a December 1995 report in Life magazine stated that 69 per cent of Americans believe in the existence of angels. In fact, Western culture also populates the universe with unseen and unseeable realities: rather than spiritual beings these are the gravitational and electromagnetic fields and forces, forces of nuclear interaction, and the other entities of contemporary natural science. Western and westernized people generally believe that these entities exist just as much as people, rocks, and chairs.

In the last few years, notwithstanding the spread of "Cocacolonization" and "MacDonaldism", the values and beliefs of Western culture have begun to encounter resistance. In the southern half of the Americas a new brand of cultural nationalism has been emerging. Latin Americans resent their dependence on North America, and also resent being receivers rather than producers of the cultural currents that shape the contemporary world. Foreign cultural domination is an agonizing issue for educated Arabs as well, who perceive it as an element of Western hegemony *vis-à-vis* their countries. Arabs find themselves at the passive end of an intercultural dialog that links them almost exclusively with Western Europe and North America.

India and the countries of South Asia had prolonged contact with British culture, but despite their admiration and assimilation of many of its traits, they have become keen on protecting their own cultural heritage. In Russia, in turn, historical experience has made for a profound ambivalence regarding Western culture, an attitude that persists to this day. Its main elements are admiration for the achievements of the West, in technology as well as in high culture, and fear that these achievements will overwhelm the Russian cultural heritage and the identity it bestows on people.

Admiration mixed with fear are also hallmarks of the cultures of the young nations of sub-Saharan Africa who, though avid consumers of industrial culture, are increasingly intent on fortifying their cultural heritage. While the poor segment of the populations remains steeped in traditional beliefs and ways of life, the small élite of intellectuals searches for the roots of African racial identity, and the still smaller élite of political leaders is concerned with reinforcing their own people's national identity.

Contrasts with the Western ways of seeing oneself and the world, though not always recognized, surface almost everywhere. Latin Americans, for example, have a more highly developed sense of spirituality than the people of North America. This has historical roots: the transcendentalist elements of Latin culture date back to the 15th century. Throughout the South American continent the Catholic scholasticism of the European Middle Ages was more than a monastic philosophy: it was a cognitive system intrinsic to state and society, and it governed every aspect of life. Latin people were taught that happiness is tied to the sacred vehicle of grace, which in turn is the exclusive prerogative of the Catholic Church. Not surprisingly, subservience to ecclesiastical authority, like subservience to God and King, became axiomatic in the morality of everyday life. Even when the colonial epoch drew to a close, no accommodation took place between the scholastic legacy and modern scientific thought. Anglo-Saxon pragmatism, rooted in the application of the concepts and methods of the natural sciences to the material spheres of life, has never taken hold in the Latin parts of the hemisphere.

Though in a different form, transcendentalism is also a feature of the Hindu and the Buddhist cultures of the Indian subcontinent; in the Muslim culture it combines with monotheism and mysticism. The indigenous cultures of black Africa have always been both spiritualist and animistic, and these elements have never been eliminated, not by the zeal of Christian missionaries nor the marketing propaganda of transnational corporations.

The Oriental mind conserves many aspects of its traditional beliefs. The great cultural circle that radiated from China during the last millennium was shaped by the naturalism of Lao Tse, the social discipline of Confucius, and the Buddha's concern with personal enlightenment. In the 20th century these cultural origins branched in different directions, giving rise to the orthodox culture of Mao's Yanan, the pragmatic culture of Hong Kong's Kong-Tai, and the mix of naturalism, Confucianism, and Buddhism that characterizes the culture of contemporary Japan. The Kong-Tai and Japanese branches of the Chinese cultural tradition maintain a penchant for all things concrete and practical, so it is unsurprising that societies where these strong traditions have long held sway have no difficulty in adopting, or even improving upon, Western technology. These cultures became "modernized", but they did not become westernized. Their own brand of modernism remains culturally specific — the very reason why Oriental work habits and group loyalties cannot be readily transplanted to Europe and to America.

Finding unity in the diversity

Finding ways for all these different cultures to live and evolve together on a small and interdependent planet is a major challenge. Clearly, each culture needs to evolve in its own right, respecting its roots and traditions yet growing toward the values and visions that would permit its people to live in harmony with other cultures as well as with nature. This is a basic requirement. Peace in the world community is threatened more by the clash of cultures than by the intransigence of nation-states.

In a rapidly shrinking and globally interdependent world, it is likely that the societies of the Western cultural sphere would find themselves in head-on confrontation with Islamic, Orthodox Christian, Japanese, Chinese, Latin, and other cultures that hold values and visions different from those of Western Christianity. The Balkan hot-spot illustrates the cogency of such a scenario. When the Ottomans entered Bosnia in the 15th century, the two cultures that arose in the Balkans following Constantine's division of the Roman Empire — the Roman Catholic and the Greek Orthodox — were joined by a third: Islam. Since then, these three cultures have clashed time and time again. Following the fading of the power of Tito's unification of Yugoslavia under the banner of Communism, their mutual intolerance produced the blood-baths of the 1990s.

Yet the scenario of "the West and the rest" is not the only possibility. In matters regarding the environment and a host of other issues, people of this global world's many diverse cultures have common interests. It is to their advantage not to let their culturally diverse values and goals obscure the areas where their interests coincide. More effective and responsible use of the new information and communications systems is essential for positive development of the world's cultures. Modern communications cannot only link people within a given culture, but also link different cultures. Closer links would mitigate animosity, reducing the potential for conflict and reinforcing mutual understanding. They would help people in different cultures to discover common interests, opening the way toward harmonious goals and objectives.

However, formidable obstacles stand in the way of a free flow of information across the globe. Journalists reporting on issues and stories which are potentially embarrassing to the local sources of power are threatened, harassed, arrested, beaten, kidnapped, and even murdered. Outspoken press and communication facilities are banned or destroyed. IFEX, the International Freedom of Expression and Exchange Network, receives more than 1,500 complaints annually from journalists, and issues an average of 1,000 alerts; it also receives nearly 500 complaints on violations of media outlets including occupation of premises, arson and bombing attacks, suspensions, prohibitions, censorship, and financial and judicial pressure. These complaints are likely to be merely the tip of the iceberg; the vast majority of the offenses are not reported for fear of reprisals.

A muzzled press fails to reach the reality of grassroots existence. In many parts of the developing world simple people, especially women, have no access to the media. African and Latin American women work in the fields and have their babies at home; they scarcely venture out of a closed society and hardly anybody seeks their opinion. Under these circumstances the enormous potential of today's globe-circling communication networks to bring people closer remains tragically unexploited.

Access to the media for ordinary people, and the freedom and willingness of the media to report on their concerns, hopes and worries, are crucial to creating better understanding among peoples and cultures. Unity in cultural diversity can only be discovered and effectively embraced if people know of each other, recognize shared concerns, and discover cooperative ways they can pursue common goals. People and cultures need to grow beyond the stage of animosity to the stage of mutual tolerance — and then to the stage of active and mutually beneficial cooperation. For this growth to occur, understanding born of contact and achieved through communication is essential.

Cooperation based on understanding and mediated by communication could lift the contemporary world beyond the stage of coexistence to a new and higher level. It could open the way toward a culture of interexistence.[*] Interexistence means active, participatory relationships, instead of intolerant, or even merely tolerant ones. It calls for living not just side by side, but with each other, overcoming ignorance and hostility, transcending dogmatism and fundamentalism.

In earlier societies, as in animal groups, a level of intolerance and hostility had a functional role. It established relationships between individuals, reinforcing a definite pecking order. Between groups, it defined territories within which biological blood-lines could be propagated and traditional values and lifeways handed down. Other tribes were either immaterial to a group's existence — and if so, the group was mostly indifferent to them — or they were actually a threat to it, in which case it defended itself by exhibiting hostility. It was only after the introduction of agriculture and pastoralism, when people first came to live in settled communities, that neighboring tribes began to join together to form towns and villages. Then, however, intolerance and hostility were transferred to towns, states, and empires beyond the confines of the community. In the world at large, intolerance was mitigated only by the force of arms. Even Pax Romana, which in its time brought together the peoples of the known continents, was based more on the power of Rome than on the voluntary tolerance of its subjugated provinces.

In our own day, intolerance expressed through hostility can have dangerous consequences. Hostilities may exist between states separated by continents, with quite different economic and political structures, and different systems of belief. These states may be led by individuals who are confrontational by nature, and unable to comprehend the consequences of their actions. They may decide to make use of the military apparatus at their command, with awesome technologies for killing and destruction. The resulting conflict could lead to the annihilation of both victor and vanquished — and the decimation of all populations in the region.

Shifting from intolerance to tolerance among peoples and states near and far is in the common interest. But tolerance, hallmarked by a mere willingness to coexist, is not enough. Whether any of us wants it, or is even conscious of it, in today's world peoples and societies form an interacting and interdependent multiregional or global system, penetrated by the constant, and constantly growing, exchange of information, energy, resources, and people. No state is truly autonomous any more; none can ignore the potentials, processes, and demands of its neighbors. Within certain areas, the strands of interdependence reach mainly to the level of continents and subcontinents. But in other domains, those such as finance, production, trade, and technology, interdependence extends over the globe.

A world-level shift has become imperative: from passive co-existence to active interexistence. It is already getting under way. Its advance signs are the many cooperative and networking arrangements of business corporations, and the multilateral agreements and alliances of states. Businesses, states, and entire cultures are becoming dependent on each other for economic development, ecological welfare, and economic, social, and territorial security. For this reason personal and social relations between peoples and cultures, as well as political relations between states, and commercial relations among enterprises, are being revisioned and reformed. The shift to interexistence needs to be sustained and empowered. The protagonists must be clear that their relationships need to be governed by a participatory logic. The dominant logic can no longer be "I *or* you", "we *or* they", but "you *and* I", "they *and* we". The zero-sum "I win, you lose" game of adversaries must be replaced by the positive-sum "I win, you win" game of partners. As long as the players see each other's interests as merely offsetting each other, the win of one is the loss of the other (therefore the sum of the wins and losses will always equal zero). But when the players perceive that they are partners pursuing superordinate goals, they will come to realize that their interests coincide. Then they begin to play games where the sum of the wins and losses is positive: where one player wins, so does the other.

There are many such games: the principal ones concern peace and security, family planning, economic development, and a healthy environment. The way to play them is to do away with nuclear, biological, chemical, and all the deadly varieties of conventional weapons, and create instead a joint peace-keeping system. It is necessary to have fewer children in rapidly growing high-fertility populations; to share useful skills, technologies, and capital with poorer or less developed partners; to channel maximum possible investment into education, communication, and human resource development as well as to the building of basic economic and social infrastructures; and to respect the balances and thresholds that are vital to the integrity of nature.

There are positive-sum games even in such traditionally conservative areas as finance. Microcredits — loans that are sometimes as small as five dollars — have been pioneered by organizations such as the Grameen Bank of Bangladesh and the Self Employed Women's Association of India. They have already helped eight million families in all parts of the world, and are expected to help up to a hundred million by the year 2005. The Grameen Bank, for example, has been granting one-year loans averaging $120 to help people start their own business — acquire a cow, buy a sewing machine. To date, over 98 per cent of the loans have been repaid thanks to a simple but effective arrangement. A peer group of borrowers is brought together to examine plans for repayment and assume responsibility for effecting it. The group chooses its own members, examines and approves their individual projects, keeps financial records, and helps with repayments. It puts the win-win strategy of interexistence into effective practice.

The participatory logic of interexistence can create a basis for perceiving, and making good use of, complementarities which are inherent in the diversity of today's cultures, peoples, nations, and businesses. This is in everyone's shared interest. In a multicultural and interdependent world it is suicidal to maintain an intolerant attitude, and insufficient merely to espouse tolerance. The shift from a culture of confrontation and coexistence to a culture of participation and interexistence is urgent and imperative.

[1] I wish to thank Peter Seidel for recalling to me this incident.

[2] The responsibilities associated with each of these roles are spelled out in the Manifesto of The Club of Budapest, of which the full text is attached in the Annex to this Report.

[3] At the request of managers, The Club of Budapest offers its services in convening and advising Total Responsibility Councils. Further details are in the Annex, in the listing of the Projects of The Club of Budapest.

[4] A more detailed description of interexistence is given in Ervin Laszlo, *The Choice: Evolution or Extinction,* Tarcher Putnam, New York, 1994.

PART THREE

CREATIVE PATHS OF HUMAN EVOLUTION

T*he epochal challenges that confront us are numerous and diverse and, in one way or another, they call for new insights, new ethics, and a great deal of human creativity. For this reason, they call for a new vision:*

- *The vision to provide creative, adequately remunerated and meaningful jobs for all people who need them and are willing to work.*
- *The vision to temper our collective quest for economic and material growth with a quest for social justice, cultural development, and a sustainable and healthy environment.*
- *The vision to moderate our individual egoistic drives and appetites with the global ethic of living in ways that others could live as well.*
- *The vision to create social, economic, and political systems that can fulfil the needs of their people without undermining the integrity of their life-sustaining environment.*
- *The vision to rethink the priorities of development so as to reduce the huge and still growing disparity between the world's rich and poor peoples.*
- *The vision that could enable governments and public bodies to perceive, and act upon, the emerging requirements of regional and global policy development and implementation.*
- *The vision to define and create a lasting system of local, national, and global security without numerous armaments and military establishments.*

• *The vision sustainably and equitably to manage the use and enjoyment of the natural resources that are the collective patrimony of the world's peoples and nations.*

• *The vision to make social and environmental accountability part and parcel of the mission of public and private institutions and the culture of local businesses and global companies.*

• *The vision to go beyond no-holds-barred competition in zero-sum "I win, you lose" games toward competition within the framework of cooperative actions aimed at shared benefits through positive-sum "I win, you win" games.*

• *The vision to evolve a holistic approach to food production and distribution, health care and social welfare, beyond the dictates of purely short-term economic logic.*

• *The vision to appreciate, and make productive use of, the social and cultural diversity of the contemporary world in the pursuit of common goals and objectives.*

These "visions" share a basic trait: not only do they focus on the forest and not just the trees, but they see the forest as far more than merely a set of trees one next to the other. They perceive the forest as a systemic, integrated whole in which all trees, as all things, are organically linked and are thus evolving — or devolving — together. The vision of an interconnected, whole-system world is not naive utopia, nor mere speculation; it is the vision emerging at the leading edge of the contemporary natural and human sciences, anticipated and completed by the vision coming to the fore in art and literature, in deep religious and spiritual experience, and in emerging alternative and youth cultures. Its importance for our life and future cannot be overemphasized. Not only can this vision help us resolve the crisis of meaning that is penetrating more and more aspects of life as traditional as well as modern worldviews lose their power to provide a coherent and compelling image of our world and our place in it, it can also function as a large-scale map for helping us find our way to the complex and interdependent, yet enormously potent and promising, world that awaits us at the dawn of the third millennium.

CHAPTER 8

A NEW VISION FOR OUR TIME

Over the last three centuries Western civilization has divested itself of feelings of oneness with nature and empathy with other people and societies. But this period is an exception in the long and varied history of civilization, and it is now drawing to a close. The pragmatic rationality of the Occident had its uses; it would not have survived for centuries had it not. It gave societies that subscribed to it unprecedented technological powers, and apparent mastery over other people, other species, and the natural environment. Today, the legitimacy and effectiveness of this rationality is waning; the epoch of diminishing returns has arrived. Persisting in the ways that created the 20th century world would spell the decline, and ultimately the breakdown, of this world.

This is at the core of the challenges we face. We cannot survive as we are; we need new insights, new values — a more timely vision. We have powerful resources at our disposal for achieving it.

RESOURCES FOR REVISIONING

(1) Science

Breakthroughs in biotechnologies enlarge our food supply, extend our life span, and provide fresh cures to the many diseases that inflict the human condition; innovations in microelectronics open the information superhighway to global traffic, and place more information at the fingertips of the average household than was stored in the entire Vatican library in the Middle Ages. The applications of communication and control technologies enable people to reduce working hours and increase leisure time, and convey ideas and images on practically everything in every conceivable field of interest from local gossip to global crises; transport technologies make for massive streams of tourists, allowing people to travel anywhere on the six continents in a matter of hours in considerable comfort and safety; high energy technologies defy gravity, harness the power of the atom, and explore outer space and the domain of the atom.

Paradoxically, even the absence of all-out war is due in some measure to advances in high-energy physics: today's weapons have become so powerful that they endanger the potential victors themselves, reducing the spoils of war to heaps of rubble that may be poisoned and radioactive to boot.

In the minds of the general public there is no question that science has become a major — perhaps *the* major — force shaping the world. This is true, but not just for the reasons that are uppermost in the mind of the public. Atomic power, intercontinental and space travel, miracle drugs, and instant communication are technological spin-offs of science, and they do shape the world in which we live. Science is more than technology, however: it is also meaning and knowledge — at its best, genuine insight into the nature of things. These elements also shape our world. They do so through the vision we have of ourselves and the universe. Whether we know it or not, this vision influences our perceptions, colors our feelings, and impacts on our assessment of individual worth and social merit. It enters into the set of ideas, emotions, values, and ambitions that makes up our consciousness.

In these times of critical change and epochal challenge, the vision of the world underlying the latest developments in science cannot be neglected. It must become part of the world-picture of business and political leaders, media personalities and opinion-makers, and women and men in all walks of life.

This is not the case today. Today's purportedly scientific vision is obsolete and misleading. Science appears to provide a dehumanized picture of the world, dry and abstract, reduced to numbers and formulae. It seems to see the universe as a soulless mechanism, and life as no more than a random accident. The specific features of living species appear to result from a succession of accidental events in the history of biological evolution. The features of human individuals themselves are seen as a fortuitous combination of the genes with which they were born. The psyche, in turn, seems dominated by elemental drives for self-gratification so that, if people were not afraid of societal repercussions, and controled by parental and societal injunctions embedded in their unconscious, they would kill and steal, commit incest, and engage in promiscuous sex. As it is, they seem to be committed only to their own interests, indifferent to all that lies beyond their body and the ego that inhabits it.

The vision of the avant-garde sciences is vastly different. The popular ideas of Newton, Darwin, and Freud, the basic sources for today's dominant views of man and universe, have been overtaken by new discoveries. In light of the emerging insights the universe is not a lifeless, soulless aggregate of inert chunks of matter; it resembles a living organism more than it does a dead rock. Life is not a random accident, and the basic drives of the human psyche include far more than the drive for sex and self-gratification.

In the new conception there is no categorical divide between the physical world, the living world, and the world of mind and consciousness. New fields of inquiry link disciplinary domains that were hitherto separated. Quantum biology links quantum physics and the life sciences; the gap between physics and the cognitive sciences is bridged by quantum brain theory and quantum consciousness research. Insights gathered in fields such as systems and evolutionary theory, cybernetics, and chaos theory, apply equally to physical, biological, psychological, and sociological phenomena.

Interdisciplinary research programs trace the evolution of nature's great domains, and their transformation into successively emerging systems and phenomena. Cosmogenesis traces the evolution of the universe from (or perhaps only through) the Big Bang to the present and on to an as yet uncertain time horizon. Geogenesis traces the evolution of the planet's physical environment through its five billion years of existence. Biogenesis traces the evolution of life on Earth from its inception in the molecular soup of primeval oceans to its current richness and diversity. Anthropogenesis traces the evolution of hominid species within the family of the higher primates. Noogenesis, in turn, traces the evolution of the human brain from its animal origins to today's organ of meaning and consciousness; and culturegenesis traces the evolution of the cultural traits and expressions of human groups from the Australopithecines to modern *sapiens sapiens*.

In the emerging vision of science, matter, life, and mind are consistent elements within an overall process of great complexity yet coherent and harmonious design. Space and time are united as the dynamic background of the observable universe; matter is vanishing as a fundamental feature of reality, retreating before energy; and continuous fields are replacing discrete particles as the basic elements of an energy-bathed universe. The universe is a seamless whole, evolving over eons of cosmic time and producing conditions where life can emerge, and then mind. Life is an intimate web of relations that evolves in its own right, interfacing and integrating its myriad diverse elements. The biosphere is born within the womb of the universe, and mind and consciousness are born in the womb of the biosphere. Nothing is independent of any other thing, harmony is pervasive.

Our body is part of the biosphere and it resonates with the web of life on this planet. Our mind is part of our body, in touch with other minds as well as the biosphere. This is the new vision, and it is powerful — as powerful as any myth of the past and more adapted to our times. It is also incomparably more reliable, the fruit of careful observation and painstaking experiment. Yet most of us remain under the sway of myths and illusions inherited from previous generations, leading self-centered lives and seeking our interests as if they were distinct from, or even contrary to, the interests of the world around us. The consequences include tooth-and-claw competition, chauvinism and egotism, the intolerance of cultural and racial differences, insensitivity to suffering and deprivation, alienation and loneliness, and disregard for the processes and balances of nature.

Chuang Tzu, an ancient Chinese sage, wrote, "Heaven, Earth and I are living together, and all things and I form an inseparable unity." In turn, Native American Chief Seattle declared, "This we know. All things are connected like the blood which unites one family. All things are connected. Whatever befalls the Earth befalls the sons of the Earth." Many contemporary scientists share this intuition. They ask, as did Gregory Bateson, "What pattern connects the crab to the lobster and the orchid to the primrose and all four of them to me? And me to you?" And they find answer after answer in observation after observation, experiment after experiment. This, however, is not generally known. The "scientific"

worldview held by most people is half a century or more behind
the thinking and the vision of the leading researchers. This lag is
both unnecessary and undesirable.

The reasons for the worldview lag are not difficult to find.
Science's new vision is not effectively diffused, nor indeed is it
properly articulated. Pathbreaking experimental and theoretical
scientists write mainly for specialized colleagues; their expositions
are quasi-unintelligible for investigators even on neighboring
fields. There is a lingering snobbishness which maintains that writing for the public is unworthy of a serious researcher; "populariza-
tions" are to be left to publicists and journalists. Even this could
help reduce the worldview lag, but by the time new theories and
conceptions gain sufficient acceptance by scientists to prompt
efforts at popularization, popular accounts report on semi-obsolete
facts and concepts: front-line research has moved on. A similar
delay invests the writing of textbooks for introductory and general
science courses. With regard to the communication of the new
insights of science to society, there is a general but dismal rule: the
up-to-date is unintelligible, and the intelligible is obsolete.

Making the up-to-date intelligible is an urgent mission that is
almost entirely ignored by the people whose job it is to analyze
and make sense of scientific findings and accomplishments: the
philosophers and sociologists of science. For the most part they are
busy fighting "paradigm wars" and "science wars," slugging it out
between the champions of the classical view that science searches
for, and ultimately finds, objective truth based on indisputable fact,
and the more sceptical view that science is but a human institution
run by money and motivated by all-too-familiar goals such as personal advancement and professional prestige. While each side may
have a point, in these wars the essential achievement of the new
sciences is lost: their capacity to convey deep and tested — even if
not "ultimate" or "definitive" — insights into the nature of the
world, and of ourselves in the world.

Snobbish introversion among scientists, and narrow infighting
among the academic observers of science, creates a pernicious gap
between the meanings that emerge at the creative edge of science
and the concepts and ideas that dominate the mind of the public.
Reducing this gap is important for all people, especially leaders in
business and politics: their decisions affect the lives of present and
future generations, and their minds are subtly influenced by what
they understand of science. Consequently, executives in business

and leaders in politics need to be well informed, not only of science's technological spin-offs, but also of the meaning and implications of the latest theories.

Helping people to catch up with the world picture of front-line science is a moral responsibility for everybody who is concerned with, or about, the role of science in society. Scientists and the philosophers of science need to realize that science is not only a source of technology, and not only of concern to their specialized communities: it is also a source of meaning and a guide to life, and as such of concern to everyone. Science administrators, science journalists, and the media as a whole, share the responsibility for effectively communicating the emerging insights. The responsibility is also shared by educators at all levels, from the kindergarten through graduate school and adult education.

The concepts of the new vision can be communicated through various and diverse forms of presentation:

• as illustrated tales of cosmos, life, and mind for children;

• as textbooks on the scientific worldview in elementary and middle schools;

• as reference works on the new sciences in colleges and universities;

• as information briefs on the nature and dynamics of societal and environmental processes for business and political leaders;

• as fascinating discoveries on the nature of the world around us for the general public.

Popular accounts of the emerging insights can be printed as text; recorded on CD-ROM; placed on the Internet; and adapted to the latest multimedia technologies. They lend themselves to being made into documentaries, and as dramas for theater and television.

(2) Art and religion

A diffusion and legitimation of science's vision is one way we could promote the evolution of a new consciousness, but there are also many other means for attaining this end: the field of cultural creativity as a whole is implicated. "High" culture of art, literature, religion, and the spiritual domains could be a momentous force, helping people and societies develop their perceptions and evolve their consciousness. In great art and literature, and in the foundations of the spiritual experience, we can experience a deep source of inspiration for living and loving, and harmony with nature. Art, literature, and spiritual teaching can help our eyes to see, our ears to hear, and our mind to absorb the new realities unfolding in our changing times. Their message can penetrate beyond our intellect to reach our hearts.

Art is not limited to museums, galleries, and concert halls but is omnipresent in society. In its truest and finest form it shapes cities through architecture and urban design; enters our feelings through music; entertains, challenges, and informs through film, radio and television, and catalyzes comprehension through literature and drama. It is human creativity *par excellence*. Despite its different modes of expression and its own criteria of excellence, it is nourished by the same fundamental source as science: insight into the nature of human experience. The artist and the writer, rather than penetrating the microcosmos of the atom or the macrocosmos of interstellar space, penetrate the deep regions of their own psyche to find communal links with their fellow women and men, with their suffering and joy, ambitions and yearnings.

Great works of art and literature transcend the geographical place and historical time of their creators; they attain universality. They socialize us into the human community, giving us insight into the relations that bind us to each other, and to nature. Achieving the true potential of art, literature, and the diverse forms of their expression and manifestation may be crucial for our future.

With a renewed search for meaning in society, the spiritual domains of experience also gain fresh relevance. Beyond rationality, and beyond even esthetic experience, there is room, and indeed need, for genuine spiritual experience. People need to sense a union with a presence that is larger than themselves, higher and deeper than the manifest universe. As William James and other philosophers and theologians noted, in its deepest and purest form the religious experience conveys such an intuition.

That the great religions have lost much of their power and legitimacy in the eyes of modern people is not due to the obsolescence of the inspiration that gave rise to them. The original intuitions were ineffable, difficult to express in words meaningful for other people, especially people in different times and different cultures. Not surprisingly, the sacred scriptures of the religions were subject to misinterpretation and dogmatization. Over time religious communities became more concerned with the letter of the scriptures than with the spirit. The devout Christian, Jew, or Mohammedan became convinced that he could earn a place in Paradise by regularly and punctually performing religious rituals, following rules such as not eating pork or requiring his wife to wear a veil, and believing unquestioningly whatever is written in the sacred texts and interpreted by its priests. The fact that the rites and rituals would serve primarily to remind and motivate followers to lead a moral life, love their fellows, and care for the less fortunate, has tended to escape attention.

Religious leaders who are more eager to convert the heathen, and safeguard the purity of their religion, rather than to impart the spirit of their religion's founders, use the sacred scriptures to convince people that by accepting them they can enter on the unique path to assured salvation. Not only do they emphasize the rightness of the given path, they insist on the wrongness of all other paths. This "exclusivist" interpretation of the teachings allows religious communities to maintain their identity, but can lead to internecine and interreligious conflict, even fanaticism and bloodshed.

Preoccupation with rites and rituals, and competition between different faiths, must not be allowed to displace the sense of oneness, and the wonder and the humility, that accompany deep religious and spiritual experience. Such experience testifies that we are an integral part of the universe, suffused of the same primeval forces that created the world at large. As naturalist-theologian Thomas Berry wrote, it leads to the realization that the divine is intrinsic to all things, from atoms to galaxies; that the cosmos is our primary sacred community. Though Eastern in its origins, this concept is present in Christianity as well — for example, in the naturalism of St. Francis of Assisi and the evolutionism of Jesuit biologist Pierre Teilhard de Chardin. It is especially important in the practical context of the contemporary world, for it can help people move from an uncaring exploitation of the environment toward behavior characterized by what Albert Schweitzer termed "reverence for nature".

Refocused by the new spirituality and divested of the dogmatic encrustations of centuries, the great religions could return to the basic source of their inspiration. They could perform the function given by their name — *re-ligare*: binding together. Contemporary women and men deeply need to be bound to each other and to nature, with voluntary but morally compelling ties.

(3) Alternative and youth cultures

Alternative and youth cultures have been emerging in large numbers in the past few decades, but they are viewed with mistrust if not actual distaste by mainstream society. They are labeled with names such as esoterism, drug cults, New Age, and the like. This enables conservative people to dismiss the phenomenon without giving it a great deal of further thought. Doing so, however, is to throw out the baby with the bathwater. While there is undoubtedly a lunatic edge to this vast movement that is escapist, introverted, and narcissistic, there is also a core that is intensely significant and hopeful in regard to motivating social change. It indicates the emergence of a different mind-set: the evolution of a new vision. This deserves to be facilitated and empowered.

Many young people and sensitive individuals are appalled by what they consider to be the heartless impersonality and mindless destructiveness of establishment society. The rise of inner-city deprivation and violence; the drift toward anarchy, and the impotence of police and military measures to cope with it; the dissolution of the social contract between society and the worker, and the rise of unemployment and homelessness, affect the thinking, the values, and the beliefs of an increasing number of people. The range of their reactions includes addiction to drugs and adherence to esoteric cults. But it also includes serious soul-searching and a commitment to alternative beliefs, values, and lifestyles.

At the significant core of the emerging cultures some of the most entrenched beliefs of the industrial age are questioned:

• Is competition still the royal road to success — would cooperation not produce better results?

• Is it still true that efficiency is the maximum productivity for people and machines — could it be that efficiency lies in producing humanly needed and socially useful goods and services?

• Is the accumulation of wealth, and the material goods that money can buy, the true mark of a person's worth — would not some traits that money cannot buy, such as gentleness, wisdom, and caring, be the real marks of human excellence?

• Are those who survive necessarily the ones who are the strongest — could it not be that the survivors are the wisest and most synergistic with others around them?

• Could it be that the basic feminine values of nurturing, caring, and relating are actually the best antidotes to the indifference, self-centeredness, and chronic aggression that prevail in today's society?

A growing number of programs and practices exhibit and convey the new mentality. A survey by the Pathfinder Project of the California Institute of Noetic Sciences noted the following:

• Programs from the local to the global level that promote the reduction of fertility rates and thus the growth of populations;

• Programs fostering self-governance in the public, private, and independent sector organizations in the developing world;

• Multiple-stakeholder collaborative problem-solving practices in organizations and communities, leading to a growing participation of people in revitalized civil society;

• The promotion of ecologic-economic sustainability by public sector organizations and private sector businesses through policies and processes that bring economic activity into alignment with the principles of natural systems;

• Steps toward agricultural reform and sustainable agricultural practices through the conversion of vast agricultural holdings to family and cooperative farms serving local markets through bio-intensive methods and the recycling of organic wastes;

• Society-wide programs that discourage mindless consumption and acquisitive materialism, promoting in their place the values of frugality and voluntary simplicity;

• New systems of indicators that provide comprehensive forward-looking measures of societal health and wellbeing;

• Innovative partnerships in the public, private, as well as independent sectors to provide opportunities for creative work capable of serving the common good and fostering a sense of purpose;

• Multiple initiatives to change social incentive systems — through taxes, legislation, regulation, subsidies, and the like — oriented toward discouraging excessive resource use and distinguishing between investment and speculation;

• Policies and programs that facilitate a shift in attitudes and practices concerning crime and war, focusing on legitimated constraint rather than legitimated violence;

• "Noetic" technologies that foster creativity, promote community building, and nurture a broad range of human potentials;

• Education programs in groups and organizations concerned with the principles and practices of transformative learning;

• An increasingly rich menu of transformationally oriented programming in socially responsible information and communication media;

• Partnerships in the public, private, and independent sectors to support citizens in physically rebuilding their neighborhoods, communities, or cities;

• Programs that foster a spirit of service and provide opportunities for volunteers to contribute to the creation of a better world;

• The current spiritual renaissance outside traditional religious institutions even as the religious traditions themselves focus on developing a shared vision of humanity's spiritual heritage and potential.

The common focus of such programs and policies is the aspiration to create a home for humanity within nature; to achieve effective local and global self-organization; and to revitalize spiritual practice and the sense of spiritual community. The segment of the population that shares such aspirations is growing. According to the "American Lives" survey carried out by Paul Ray, it already comprises 44 million individuals, some 24 per cent of the adult population (50 per cent more women than men). Their consciousness is hallmarked by a wider range of problem perception, a higher standard of spirituality, personal development, authenticity and relationships, and greater tolerance for the views of other people.

The shift in consciousness is becoming well documented. Duane Elgin of the San Anselmo Indicators Project examined the most relevant comprehensive US and global surveys of the past decade with regard to the following questions:

• is the global communications revolution fostering a new global consciousness?

• what is the extent of humanity's global ecological awareness and concern?

• is there a shift underway toward postmodern social values?

• is a new kind of experiential or first-hand spirituality emerging?

• is there a shift underway toward more sustainable ways of living?

Elgin found that an "integral culture" is emerging, and this new culture is bridging differences, connecting people, harmonizing efforts, and discovering higher common ground. Its elements include global ecological awareness, evolving values, sustainable living, the evolution of a global brain through globe-spanning communication systems, and increasing experiential spirituality as people seek a better understanding and a more meaningful synthesis. He concluded that "a new global culture and consciousness have taken root... a shift in consciousness as distinct and momentous as that which occurred in the transition from the agricultural era to the industrial era roughly three hundred years ago."

Though California is a hotbed of youth and alternative cultures, kindred shifts in consciousness are surfacing elsewhere, too. They are most pronounced with respect to environmental issues. "The Environmental Monitor", a 1997 survey by a Canadian Research Institute, found that 70 to 90 per cent of the 27,000 people it polled on five continents were "concerned" or "very concerned" about the environment. The most concerned were in Australia, New Zealand, China, the United States,

Canada, and, surprisingly, in some developing countries. There is a parallel shift in regard to consumption patterns and lifestyles, though this is confined largely to the industrialized world. The Trends Research Institute of New York called the movement toward "voluntary simplicity in lifestyles" one of the top ten trends of 1997. Originating in the United States, this movement has spread to Europe, Australia, and Canada. Masses of people, the Institute noted, are beginning to embrace the belief that they can enhance the quality of their lives by cutting back on the quantity of products they consume.

Movements which embrace an ecological, lifestyle, and social-values orientation, are championed by voluntary associations, non-governmental organizations, community groups, nonprofit organizations, and informal networks. They are all intent on translating the values that emerge in the new cultures into practical projects oriented toward grass-roots communities, the mass media, local and global businesses, and local or national government.

Without question, a new vision is emerging at the creative margins of society. Yet serious questions remain. How contagious is this vision — how fast will it spread in societies rich and poor, westernized as well as traditional? How influential is it? Will it impact in time on the ways businesses set priorities and governments design policies, and on how mainstream society lives and acts? On this score there are grounds for concern. With few exceptions governments and businesses still place economic growth above concern with quality of life and long-term sustainability; and in the population as a whole, materialist values still dominate. Nothwithstanding a shift in consciousness in the alternative and youth cultures, and the dramatic rise of environmental awareness in various segments of society, parochialism, provincialism, self-centeredness, and tunnel vision have not been overcome in mainstream society.

When all is said and done, one fact must be faced. While popular culture, like avant-garde art and cutting-edge science, may be in a ferment, mainline public opinion is clinging to a comparatively conservative outlook. Few parts of the world are ready to embrace a vision that suggests new goals and values, especially if these seem to be asking for changes and sacrifices in patterns of consumption, professional ambitions, or the pursuit of power and wealth.

CHAPTER 9

CONCLUSIONS: WHAT REMAINS TO BE DONE

A new direction must be found for our collective evolution, departing from the one which has hallmarked the course taken by Western civilization for the past 300 years. We can no longer afford to let habit and inertia guide our steps; henceforth our evolution must be conscious. For conscious evolution, however, we must evolve our own consciousness.

The goal: conscious evolution

Vast systemic processes hold sway in the development of society, just as in the evolution of nature. They drive fundamental change, whether we know it or not. But if we ignore their underlying dynamics, we cannot consciously interact with them. It has become an urgent necessity for us to develop a higher level of evolutionary literacy.

The sciences of systems and evolution — cybernetics, general system theory, the theory of dynamical systems (chaos theory), and general evolution theory among others — tell us that, whatever their nature, complex systems evolve with an underlying logic of their own. This evolution is nonlinear but not haphazard. It has an underlying direction, a probability that certain kinds of states and conditions will come about in the wake of any basic transformation.

Today, we live in an epoch of critical thresholds, of rapid and basic transformations. Evolutionary change dynamics have become highly visible. They drive society toward greater structural complexity expressed by the convergence of the existing states and nations in new, regional, and global systems formed by their intensifying relations; toward more dynamism due to the availability (in our day through powerful technologies) of growing quantities of free energy; toward more and more complex forms of communication among the diverse parts of the system (thanks today to the new technologies of information and communication); and toward a state of potentially creative chaos, with enhanced sensitivity to other societies, as well as enterprises, cultures, and ecologies in their environment.[1]

There may not be much we can do to go counter to basic evolutionary processes; our interests lie in going with them, facilitating their unfolding. But our interests are not necessarily served by going with them blindly and indiscriminately. What good would it be if we evolved a system of interacting and interdependent societies in which there was a dictatorship of the rich and powerful; where the great majority lived at the margins of human subsistence; where nature became inhospitable and resources turned scarce; where life was harsh and competition unfettered; and where violence was rampant and might was right? Reaching such a world may be the result of an evolutionary process, but getting to it is not in our interest.

Fortunately, it is within our power to choose another path, leading toward a more livable and sustainable world. This is necessary, for the evolutionary path adopted by Western and westernized societies has reached a critical threshold. Continued movement along this path would create growing conflicts and crises, it would lead to further rich-poor polarization accompanied by mounting unemployment, starvation, epidemics and massive migrations, followed by violence and war, leading perhaps to extinction. Even extinction would not be unprecedented: innovative cultures have often overexploited their environment and faced the choice of either changing their ways, or dying out. But, with the exception of islands and other remote regions, they also had another choice: that of moving on. That choice, however, is no longer available.

Degeneration and extinction has never been an arbitrary or exceptional development: populations in nature have often become extinct — some 99 per cent of the complex species that emerged since the Cambrian era are now part of the fossil record. If this were also to be the fate of the human species it would not be contrary to the fundamental processes of evolution; it would merely be one of their less fortunate outcomes.

But humanity does not necessarily face this dismal scenario, for it has a resource at its command that is not shared by any other species that had ever populated the Earth: a conscious mind. The human mind, equipped with pronounced capacities for social organization and served by a variety of powerful technologies, would be entirely capable of guiding our further evolution. But to do so effectively its capacities would have to evolve. Not just its technologies, but its perceptions, empathies, values, and priorities.

In an address to the joint session of the US Congress on 21st February 1990, Czech writer-president Vaçlav Havel said, "Without a global revolution in the sphere of human consciousness, nothing will change for the better... and the catastrophe towards which this world is headed — the ecological, social, demographic, or general breakdown of civilization — will be unavoidable." He was right. At the same time the breakdown of civilization is not unavoidable: human consciousness can be evolved. But it still has a long way to grow.

The way: evolving our consciousness

How can we accelerate the evolution of our consciousness? It is not enough to learn more facts and figures and exercise the current rationality. To live with each other and not against each other, to live in a way that does not rob the chances of others to live as well, to care what is happening to the poor and the powerless as well as to nature — this calls for more than knowing the facts and mastering the statistics. It also calls for feeling and intuition; for sensing the situation in which we find ourselves, apprehending its manifold aspects and dimensions, and creatively responding to them. The full scope of our attention, empathy, and concern must rise from today's ego-, business-, and nation-centered dimension to a broader human-, nature-, and planet-centered one. We cannot cope with the transformation of our economic, social, and ecological systems without transforming ourselves. The way to conscious evolution is through an evolved consciousness.

In mid-century, Albert Einstein remarked that we have changed everything in the world except ourselves. Now, at the end of the century, we are further down the road: we have changed more of our world, but we have also begun to change ourselves. A more evolved consciousness is emerging in a growing number of people: artists and scientists, insightful business and opinion-leaders, spiritual people, and members of youth and alternative cultures. It is also surfacing in people who have had direct experience of oneness with others, and with nature. Prayer and meditation, and altered states of consciousness in general, motivate and facilitate this evolution. Someone who has come close to physical death experiences life in a new light, has no further fear of death, develops empathy with other people, and takes pleasure in simply living and sharing. An individual who, in an altered state of consciousness intuited the experience of someone else, knows what it is literally to become another person, feeling his or her physical sensations and experiencing his or her emotions. And someone who has had the privilege to travel in outer space and look at the Earth in its living splendor experiences an intense tie to this home planet for the rest of his days.

People who have undergone regression therapy, who have had near-death experiences, or have had the experience of space travel have a different consciousness. They have a fresh appreciation of existence and reverence for nature; they evolve deep humanitarian and ecological concerns; and they find differences among people, whether in the area of sex, race, color, language, political conviction, or religious belief, interesting and enriching rather than threatening. They realize that they cannot do anything to nature without simultaneously doing it to themselves — and that other people, whether next door, in distant parts of the world, or of generations yet to be born, are not separate from them, and their fate is not a matter of indifference.

The kind of consciousness that is essential for a conscious evolution of the contemporary world is already evolving in some people, and it can evolve in all. It can be purposefully fostered. The intuitions that give credence and substance to a new consciousness must not be suppressed, must not be screened out by a rationality that ascribes them to childish fantasy or, if persistent, to an unhinged mind. School and family must encourage children to treasure feelings and empathies that link them to other people, to humanity and to nature; the pressures of daily life and competition must leave room for intuitions, dreams, and daydreams of oneness with others and the planet. Educated people need to familiarize

themselves   with   the   emerging   vision   of
science; focus and make socially relevant the creative insights and
intuitions of the arts and religions; and foster the positive values
and visions that surface in the alternative and youth cultures.

The stakes are high. Without a new consciousness it is unlikely
that we will be able to avert deepening economic, social, and cultural conflicts and ecological breakdowns. But, if our consciousness is able to move up from the self-centered and parochial to the
planet-centered and universally human dimension, our economic
power and technological sophistication will be matched with a
deeper spiritual and emotional maturity. This is the creative
evolution we need in order to consciously evolve our world, and
bring ourselves and our children safely to a soft landing in the post-
modern age of the third millennium.

[1] For a detailed discussion of these processes, see Ervin Laszlo, *Evolution: the General Theory*, Hampton Press, NJ, 1996.

CRUCIAL INSIGHTS FROM SCIENCE

The vision that is currently emerging in the front-line sciences has an important role which is not generally suspected: to reintegrate our fragmented world-picture, giving us the necessary information as well as the inspiration to live and grow in an interconnected and complex world. The basic elements of the new vision are contained in the latest concepts and theories of matter (physical reality), of life (the biological-ecological domain), and of mind (the sphere of the human mind).

The new insights are sophisticated, yet they are not difficult to grasp. They concern the *nonmaterial foundations of physical reality* ("matter," though seemingly solid, is structured energy, interacting with the almost fathomless virtual-energy sea where it originated); *the subtle linkages of life* (all living things in the biosphere, ourselves included, are subtly yet effectively interacting); and the *newly rediscovered powers of the mind* (when in a suitably "tuned" state, our brain and consciousness can communicate with almost any aspect of human life and the natural world).

Once we have understood these insights, our whole worldview will shift. We will never again look in quite the same way at ourselves, at others, and at the wider reality which is not only the backdrop, but the active context of our existence

The nonmateriality of matter

Since the pre-Socratic thinkers of Ancient Greece, philosophers have been debating the nature of the ultimate building blocks or "stuff" of reality. The arguments crystallized around the question whether the universe is essentially material, or ideal, or possibly both. Democritus thought that it was material; Hegel that it was ideal; and Descartes that it was both material and ideal. When Marx elevated the choice into a basic premise of the socialist worldview, the debate between materialists and idealists entered the field of politics. The communist countries declared that the world was material, and those who thought differently were either naive dreamers or sinister reactionaries.

While ideological questions concerning the material basis of the world are now outdated, inquiries into the ultimate building blocks of the observable world are not. Scientists have been debating questions relating to the nature of matter throughout the 20th century. In the light of their findings, the philosophical choice between materialisn and idealism is just as outdated as its political implications. Physical reality is not necessarily divided into materialists and idealists, the concepts of the new physics transcend these simple alternatives. They do not speak directly to the reality of mind, but contest that the universe is built of basic building blocks that can be equated with any reasonable concept of matter.

Current insights as to the nature of matter did not dawn all at once; their evolution is fascinating and worth a brief summary. In the 19th century, the basic constituents of the known universe were said to be matter, space, and time. Matter was seen to occupy space and move about in it; it was the primary aspect of reality. Time, in Newton's words, was considered to flow equitably through all eternity, not interfering with the adventures of matter. Space, in turn, was seen as a backdrop or container; without the furnishings of material bodies, it was not endowed with full reality.

During the 20th century, this concept has been fundamentally revised. It was revised first in Einstein's relativistic universe, where spacetime became an integrated four-dimensional manifold, and then in Bohr's quantum mechanics, where assumptions about the observer-independent reality of any aspect of physical reality have been purposively suspended. The latest theories of the new physics suggest yet another modification. Matter, it appears, is not the primary furnishing of the physical universe. In the light of what scientists are currently learning about the nature of the quantum vacuum — the energy sea that underlies spacetime — the primary reality of the universe is energy, or, more exactly, it is the virtual energy that fills cosmic space.

The reason for the shift from matter to energy as the primary reality lies in the discovery that, notwithstanding its name, the quantum vacuum is not an empty space — a vacuum — but filled space: a plenum. It is the locus of the "zero-point field", so named because the energies of this field become manifest when all other energies vanish in a particle or system: at the zero point.

In itself, this vast "Dirac-sea" (after the English physicist Paul Dirac who first computed its parameters) is not electromagnetic, gravitational, or nuclear. Instead, it is the originating source of the known electromagnetic, gravitational, and nuclear forces and fields. It is also the originating source of the matter particles themselves. By stimulating the zero-point field of the vacuum with sufficient energy — of the order of 10^{27} erg/cm^3 — a particular region of it is "kicked" from the state of negative into the state of positive energy. This makes for "pair-creation": out of the vacuum emerges a positive energy (real) particle, with a negative energy (virtual) particle twin remaining in it.

The energy density of the zero-point field is well-nigh inconceivable. Physicist John Wheeler estimated it at 10^{27} Joules per cm^3 — which in the light of Einstein's mass-energy equation $E = mc^2$ works out to 10^{-94} gram/cm^3 (provided that quantum laws hold all the way to the so-called Planck length of 10^{-33} cm). The density of 10^{-94} gram/cm^3 signifies more energy than there is bound in matter in all the galaxies and stars of the universe — according to David Bohm, 10^{40} times more. (The matter density of the universe is a mere 10^{-24} gram/cm^3.) Fortunately, vacuum energies are "virtual." Otherwise, since energy is equivalent to mass and mass always carries gravitation, the universe would instantly collapse to a size smaller than the radius of an atom.

On first sight it would appear that the observable universe floats, as it were, on the surface of the vacuum's quasi-infinite energy sea. But because the observable universe is so much less energetic than the underlying quantum vacuum, it is not a solid condensate floating on top of it, but more like a set of bubbles suspended in it. The physical universe is not a solidification of vacuum energies, but a thinning of it — a 180° shift from the idea that matter is dense, autonomous, and moving in passive and empty space.

The quantum vacuum is a world in itself, unobservable, but not without effects on the observable realm. Through the vacuum electrons interact throughout the universe, and material (mass-energy) objects are part of the electromagnetic field created by their interaction. According to recent hypotheses, including those advanced by this writer, the electromagnetic field of the cosmos is governed by a subquantum matrix that is not electromagnetic in itself, but scalar. (Scalar waves were discovered by Nikola Tesla: they have magnitude but no directional force — no vector.) Tesla-waves propagate longitudinally — rather than transversally, as electromagnetic waves — and are not limited by the laws of wave propagation in spacetime.

The matrix created by interfering scalar waves carries information in a "holographic" form, distributed throughout spacetime. This information, called by Bohm the quantum potential, guides electromagnetic interactions (matter-like events) in the observable world. It is an interconnecting holofield, injecting information on the evolving state of the universe in each of its parts.[1]

Experimental evidence shows that the worlds of matter and the vacuum interact. Under certain conditions the vacuum's zero-point energies act on the electrons that orbit atomic nuclei. Electrons "jump" from one energy state to another, and the photons they emit exhibit the Lamb-shift — a frequency that, due to the presence of the zero-point field, is slightly shifted from its normal value. The energies of the vacuum also create a radiation pressure on two closely spaced metal plates. Between the plates some wavelengths of the vacuum field are excluded, reducing its energy density with respect to the field outside. This creates a pressure — the Casimir effect — pushing the plates inward and together.

Other interactions may also exist. Einstein's famous "relativistic effects" (such as the slowing down of clocks when accelerated close to the speed of light, and the increasing of the mass of objects at those velocities) may be due to the interaction of real world objects with the vacuum's energy field. Close to the speed of light the matter-particles (fermions) of objects rub against the force-particles (bosons) of the vacuum, and this friction slows down their processes and increases their mass. The vacuum may be a quasi-physical field that interacts with the mass-energy entities ("material" objects) that exist in space and time.

In some conceptions the vacuum's holofield has the properties of a superfluid. It is known that in supercooled helium all resistance and friction ceases; it moves through narrow cracks and capillaries without loss of momentum. Conversely, objects move through a superfluid without encountering resistance. (Electrons also move through it without resistance, so superfluids are also superconductors.) In a sense, a superconducting superfluid is not "there" for the objects that move through it — there is no friction, no resistance, no information about its presence. This can explain why we fail to register the presence of the vacuum's staggeringly dense energies with our bodily senses and even with our most sensitive instruments: the energies are superfluid with regard to our bodies and our instruments.

However, as Russian physicist Piotr Kapitza discovered, in a superfluid only those objects that are in constant quasi-uniform motion move without friction. If an object is strongly accelerated, vortices are created in the fluid, and these produce resistance: the classical interaction effects surface. Hence, when particles move uniformly, spacetime is Euclidean and approximates a superfluid; and when they are accelerated, spacetime appears curved, since the vacuum's zero-point field interacts with their motion. For these effects to become readily observable, speeds close to that of light must be achieved — in our everyday world the effects remain "subtle" — beyond the ken of ordinary sensory observation.

Front-line research in physics confirms the basic notion that underlies these theories. Current work follows up a suggestion made by physicists Paul Davies and William Unruh in the mid-1970s. Davies and Unruh based their argument on the difference between constant-speed and accelerated motion in the vacuum's zero-point field. Constant-speed motion would exhibit the vacuum's spectrum as isotropic (the same in all directions), whereas accelerated motion would produce a thermal radiation that breaks open the directional symmetry.

The hypothesis of a "Davies-Unruh effect" prompted scientists to investigate whether accelerated motion through the vacuum field would produce incremental effects. This expectation has borne fruit. It turned out that the inertial force itself could be due to interactions in that field. According to US physicists Bernhard Haisch, Alfonso Rueda and Harold Puthoff the accelerated motion of objects through the vacuum produces a magnetic field, and the particles that constitute the objects are deflected by this field. The larger the object the more particles it contains, hence the stronger the deflection — and greater the inertia. Inertia thus appears to be a form of electromagnetic resistance arising in accelerated frames from the distortion of the otherwise superfluid vacuum field.

Mass itself may be a product of vacuum interaction. If Haisch and collaborators are right, the concept of mass is neither fundamental nor even necessary in physics. When the mass-less electric charges of the vacuum (the bosons that make up the superfluid zero-point field) interact with the electromagnetic field, beyond a specific threshold of energy mass is effectively "created." In the emerging vision of the new physics mass is a structure condensed from vacuum energy, not a fundamental given in the universe.

This has a further consequence. If mass is a product of vacuum energy, so is the force of gravitation. Gravity, as we know, is always associated with mass, obeying the inverse square law (it drops off proportionately to the square of the distance between the gravitating masses). So if mass is produced in interaction with the zero point field, then the force that is associated with mass is also produced in this way. This, however, means that all the fundamental characteristics that we ordinarily associate with matter are vacuum-field interaction products: inertia, mass, as well as gravity.

In the light of these and related developments, it is reasonable to view matter as a product of the vacuum's zero-point field. In the emerging vision of the new physics, physical reality is not material. There is no "absolute matter," only an absolute matter-generating virtual-energy field.

This conclusion is consistent with what scientists have known for decades about the nature of the subnuclear domains of reality. At the ultrasmall scale matter disappears: particles no longer exist as individual entities. The atoms and molecules that make up the substances we experience as matter are various configurations of protons, neutrons, mesons, and electrons, and these in turn are configurations of quarks. Quarks, in turn, are enduring energy-patterns superimposed on the underlying zero-point field. Hence the objects we consider material are not irreducible entities moving about in space as in a passive vessel. Rather, they are critical nodes within the vacuum's potentially dynamic virtual energies.

The vacuum, rather than matter, has basic physical reality. It is a continuous medium that can form patterns and create waves. Light and sound are traveling waves in it, and tables and trees, rocks and swallows, and we human beings, are standing waves.

That matter in its ultimate nature would be nonmaterial is not new to modern physics: it was anticipated by mathematician

William Clifford a hundred years ago. In mid-century, Albert Einstein, Herman Weyl, and Erwin Schrödinger were of the same opinion. They maintained that the physical universe must be understood in terms of the geometry of space (or spacetime). Consequently, what we observe as material bodies are in reality shapes and variations in the underlying structure of space. Yet, as physicists are now coming to admit, empty space cannot have a structure; hence space — more exactly spacetime — must have physical reality of its own. It must be a continuous medium with a substructure made up of interfering patterns and configurations of waves. The emerging view is that the mass-particles that constitute seemingly solid material bodies are actually standing waves in the spacetime-filling quantum vacuum, and the photons that make up beams of light are traveling waves.

The concept of a physically real energy-medium that fills space and gives rise to matter resembles age-old intuitions of an energy-filled cosmos out of which arise all the things we know and experience. The parallel extends to the ultimate fate of matter in the universe. According to Stephen Hawking's celebrated theory of black holes, all remaining particles in the superdense core of a degenerate star "evaporate," and the surviving particles fall back into the zero-point field, much in the same way that *Prana* in Hindu cosmology vanishes back into *Akasha*.

In the early days of quantum theory, English physicist Sir Arthur Eddington was of the view that all things (even one's wife) were essentially sets of complex differential equations. We can now improve on Eddington's idea. All things of a material nature, including the atoms that make up our body, are complex standing waves in the universe's underlying holofield.

The links of life

Contrasted with the nonmateriality of matter, the shift from the habitual to the current view of the nature of life may seem modest. Yet, when compared with classic Darwinism, the standard biological worldview of the late 19th and most of the 20th century, it is just as fundamental.

Darwinists maintained a two-fold disjunction in the living realm: between the organism and the genetic information that specifies its structure, and between the organism and its external environment. They held that a corresponding two-fold chance governs the evolution of species: the chance mutations that occur in the insulated genetic pool of their members, and the chance fit of the resulting mutants with the environments in which they happen to find themselves. The genetic pool mutates randomly, and the organism it codes is exposed to a succession of independently evolving environments. In that environment natural selection weeds out the unfit mutants and allows the fit to survive and reproduce — and in time to produce further mutants.

Current observations and experiments suggest a different view of the processes of life and the dynamics of its evolution. Post-Darwinian scientists find subtle but effective links between the genome and the organism, as well as between the organism and its environment. Pure chance — which requires the absence of causal links — is not likely to hold sway anywhere in the world of the living. Indeed, chance is an unlikely explanation of the principal facts we observe.

Chance explanations are not enough to explain the earliest phases of the evolution of life on Earth. Complex structures have appeared on this planet within astonishingly brief periods of time. The oldest rocks date from about four billion years, while the earliest and already highly complex forms of life (blue-green algae and bacteria) are over 3.5 billion years old. How this level of complexity could have emerged within the relatively short period of about 500 million years lacks a satisfactory answer. Chance alone cannot account for the facts: a random mixing of the molecular soup would have taken incomparably longer to produce these structures. Failing to find a reasonable explanation, scientists such as Lord Kelvin maintained that life was very likely imported "ready-made" to Earth from elsewhere in the universe. In recent years several biologists, including DNA-decoder Sir Francis Crick, have not been averse to this idea.

Nor can unmitigated chance explain how some highly specific anatomical and structural features could be shared by plants and animals that evolved on widely different locations with entirely different evolutionary histories. The more than 250,000 species of higher plants found in almost every part of the world show only three basic forms of the distribution of leaves around the stem, and a single form (the spiral) accounts for 80 per cent of all of them. Animal species, too, have remarkably similar structural forms, though they show great variation in complexity at all levels. The wings of birds and bats, for example, are homologous with the flippers of the phylogenetically entirely unrelated seals and the forelimbs of the equally unrelated amphibians, reptiles, and verte-brates. While the size and shape of the bones show great variation, the bones themselves are similarly positioned, both in relation to each other and to the rest of the body. Diverse species also exhibit common orders in regard to the position of the heart and the ner-vous system: in endoskeletal species the nervous system is in the dorsal (back), and the heart in the ventral (front) position, while in exoskeletal species the positions are precisely reversed.

It appears that diverse species can construct nearly identical phenomes (biologically expressed organisms) on the basis of vastly different genomes (the information that is expressed in the organ-isms). Even more astonishing is the reverse case: when the same element of a genome recurs in widely different phenomes. Very similar, even identical, genes have been found in species that evolved entirely independently of one another. Swiss biologist Walter Gehring and his collaborators discovered that the three dozen or so eyes that occur in the living realm have a common origin. The reticular eye of the fly and the retina-covered visual organ of mice and men derive from the same basic pattern; indeed, they are coded by one and the same "master control gene." The genetic mechanism of the eye is interchangeable among widely differing species — the "eye-gene" of the mouse will induce the growth of an eye on the fly.

Chance alone cannot account for the plain fact that life evolved from simple prokaryotic cells and produced complex multicellular organisms. Any but the simplest forms of life manifest a staggering complexity. The assembly even of a primitive self-replicating prokaryote (primitive non-nucleated cell) involves building a dou-ble helix of DNA consisting of some 100,000 nucleotides, with each nucleotide containing an exact arrangement of 30 to 50 atoms, together with a bi-layered skin and the proteins that enable the cell to take in food. This construction requires an entire series of reactions, finely coordinated with each other. Mathematical physicist Fred Hoyle pointed out that this process occurring purely by chance is about as likely as a hurricane blowing through a scrap yard assembling a working aeroplane.

Some years earlier, Konrad Lorenz came to a similar conclusion. While it is formally correct, he said, to assert that the principles of chance mutation and natural selection play a role in evolution, by itself this cannot explain the facts. Mutations and natural selection may account for variations within given species, but the roughly four billion years available on this planet for biological evolution could not have been sufficient for chance processes to generate today's complex and ordered organisms from their protozoic ancestors. It is not enough for mutations to produce one or a few positive changes in a species; they must produce a full set. By a process of random trial and error that would take time — far more time than was available on this planet.

The evolution of feathers, for example, does not produce a reptile that can fly: radical changes in musculature and bone structure are also required, along with a faster metabolism to power sustained flight. Each innovation by itself is not likely to offer evolutionary advantage; on the contrary, it is likely to make an organism less fit than the standard form from which it departed. And if so, it would soon be eliminated in turn by natural selection. A random stepwise elaboration of the genetic code of a species is astronomically unlikely to produce viable results.

French biologist M. Schutzenberger noted that one would need an almost blind faith in Darwinian theory to believe that chance alone could have produced in the line of birds all the modifications needed to make them high-performing flying machines, or that random mutations would have led to the line of mammals after the extinction of the dinosaurs — given that mammals are a long way from dinosaurs along the axis that conduces from fish to reptiles. His Italian colleague Giuseppe Sermonti was of the same opinion. It is not credible, he said, that small random mutations and natural selection could have produced a dinosaur from an amoeba. Life cannot and does not evolve by piecemeal improvements, but through occasional massive and finely coordinated innovations.

Massive and finely coordinated innovations could hardly occur by pure chance. If there is no hidden program guiding evolution — which was the thesis of the now abandoned theory of "pre-adaptation" — then in some way the environment itself must be creating a selection pressure that limits the variability of the genome. The genome cannot be entirely isolated from the rest of the organism — and from the rest of the world.

There is experimental evidence to back up this assumption. For example, when in the laboratory particular genes of a strain of bacteria are rendered defective, some bacteria mutate back to precisely those genes that the scientists made inoperative. And when some plants and insects are subjected to toxic substances, they mutate their genome in precisely such a way as to detoxify the toxins and create resistance to them.

Rather than a haphazard recombination of genes, genetic variations appear to be flexible responses on the part of the genome to the changes successive generations of organisms experience in their milieu. The emerging insight combines a long-discredited thesis of Jean Baptiste Lamarck (that the changes the organism experiences can be inherited) with a main pillar of the theory of Charles Darwin (that inheritance is always mediated by the genetic structure of the organism). It appears that the influences an organism experiences in its milieu are indeed affecting subsequent generations — not, to be sure, because changes in the parent organism would be directly communicated to the offspring, but because some effects felt by the phenome (the organism) of the parent leave their mark on its genome (its genetic pool of information), and thus also leave their mark on its offspring.

The discovery of subtle links between the genome and the organism, and between the organism and the environment, brings important new insights regarding the nature of life. The living world is not the harsh domain of classical Darwinism, where each struggles against all, with every species, every organism and every gene competing for advantage against every other. Organisms are not skin-enclosed entities, they cannot be entirely selfish. Life evolved in what English biologist Brian Goodwin called a "sacred dance" between living organisms and their milieu. Subtle strains of that dance extend throughout the biosphere, to all the species and ecologies that inhabit it.

Links between the genome and the phenome of organisms, and between organisms and environments, mean that there are no purely isolated, chance processes in the living realm. This insight may be a shock to classical Darwinists, but would not come as a surprise to Darwin himself. In an almost forgotten passage in chapter 21 of *The Descent of Man*, Darwin wrote, "The birth both of the species and of the individual are equally parts of that grand sequence of events that our minds refuse to accept as the result of blind chance..." "The understanding", he added, "revolts at such a conclusion."[2]

The discovery of subtle links in the realms of life has important implications. Links in nature cannot exist in empty space; there must be a continuous medium that "carries" or conveys them. This medium need not be based on matter; it could also be based on energy. The paradigm for linkages of this kind is physics' set of universal fields — the electromagnetic, gravitational, and the strong and weak nuclear fields. In biology, the indicated assumption is the existence of a specific kind of field: the bio- or bioenergy field.

The bioenergy field is not a separate reality: it is an integral part of the biophysics of the organism. Life requires a set of biochemical reactions that operate under genetic control to power the metabolism of the cell, creating organic structure and determining the organism's physiological processes. Life also requires bioelectrical activity, in the form of currents of protons, electrons, and charged atoms and molecules generated by the thousands of enzyme sites within each cell. Cells are cytoelectric microcosms comprised of an ever-changing web of currents and fields powered by biochemical activity. Last but not least, life involves the activity of biomagnetic fields. These fields arise because all electric charges generate a magnetic field that rises and falls at the same frequency as the originating current. The organism's cytomagnetic fields form a complex, close-range system of energies that interact to reinforce or suppress each other, and forming beat frequencies between sources of different frequency and standing waves between sources of the same frequency.

This miraculous web of biochemical, electromagnetic and electrical processes and fields provides a clue to a puzzle that has long intrigued investigators: how an organism, consisting of a great variety of tissues and cells and a vast number of processes, can develop and function as an integrated whole. And how this whole can mobilize, in an almost inconceivably coordinated way, the free energy it needs whenever and wherever it needs it.

We should recall that the human body consists of some 1,000,000 billion cells, about 15,000 times more than people on Earth and a thousand times more than stars in the Milky Way galaxy. Of these astronomical number, 600 billion cells are dying and the same number are regenerating each day — over 10 million per second. The average skin cell lives only for about two weeks; bone cells are renewed every three months. Every 90 seconds millions of antibodies are synthesized, each from about 1,200 aminoacids; and every hour 200 million erythrocytes are regenerated. According to radio isotope analyses carried out at Oak Ridge Laboratories, 98 per cent of the atoms that make up the organism are also replaced every year. There is no substance in the body that would be constant, though heart and brain cells endure longer than most. Yet the substances that coexist at a given time produce some 10^{30} biochemical reactions each and every second.

This fabulous number and diversity of processes cannot be co-ordinated entirely via the physicochemical communication of cells and organs. Though some chemical signalling is enormously effective (for example, that of control genes) both the speed with which processes spread in the body, and the complexity of the processes themselves, mean that reliance on such signalling alone is unrealistic. The living organism is "coherent" — conditions and reactions that occur in one part also occur in another — and its coherence is not entirely ensured by hierarchy of "line managers" or control molecules whipping the "housekeeping" enzymes into shape. It is more likely based on a system-wide intercommunication that, in the words of biophysicist Mae-Wan Ho of England's Open University, is instantaneous, noiseless, and nonlocal.

Instant, noiseless, and nonlocal communication calls for a field that suffuses the entire organism. Such a field, although it informs the whole organism, does not constrain organs and organ systems to behave uniformly. The field is "factorizable", allowing relative independence for molecular and cellular subunits within the limits of the organism's overall coherence.

Evidence for the functions of the bioenergy field is accumulating. Freeman and Barrie carried out simultaneous recordings of a large area of the brain cortex of rabbits using an array of 64 electrodes and found oscillations that are coherent over the entire array. Though the amplitudes differ, the pattern of discharges is simultaneous and uniform. In turn, Italian biophysicists Giuliano Preparata and Emilio Del Giudice found that so-called Josephson junctions are present in living tissue, producing spontaneous synchronizations of the frequencies of adjacent groups of cells. And Mae-Wan Ho discovered the physical substrate responsible for such synchronizations: it is the liquid crystalline structure that extends as a mesophase throughout the organism.

The bioenergy field has measurable frequencies and radiations. Scientists at the A.S. Popov Bio-information Institute, in the former Soviet Union, found that the frequencies of the human bioenergy field fall within the range of 300 to 2,000 nanometers (billionth of a meter). Investigators at Lanzhou University and the Atomic Nuclear Institute in Shanghai discovered that its radiation varies with the mental powers of the subject. This was borne out by the work of Valerie Hunt at the Energy Fields Laboratory at UCLA. Using sophisticated equipment, both hard-wired to the test subjects and remote telemetry apparatus using short-range FM data transmission, Hunt found that the energy fields radiating from the bodies of mystics, seers and healers consistently move in a higher frequency domain (around or beyond 400 Hz) than the fields of persons in normal states of mind (the latter are usually below the 250 Hz range).

There is growing evidence that the organism's radiant bioenergy field interacts with other fields in the environment. Sensitive individuals such as healers affect others around them, as well as being affected by them. And most people are affected by some of the fields that surround them — the electric, magnetic, and electromagnetic radiations that exist in nature, as well as those that are the unintended side-effects of high voltage power lines and high-frequency transmissions of cellular telephones, among others. People are affected by subtler energies as well. Traditionally called "etheric," "mental," or "spiritual," these superfine energies emerge in the interaction of the bioenergy field of the body with low frequency and low-intensity electromagnetic, scalar, and quantum fields in the Earth's physical environment.

The body's sensitivity to subtle changes in its milieu, just as to changes in its own structure, makes human beings vulnerable to a great variety of forces and fields, from electro-smog to the aroma of flowers. This very sensitivity, however, opens the possibility to redress imbalances that occur within the body. It provides the premise for bioenergy medicine, a kind of healing traditionally well known in the East, in Indian (Ayurvedic), Tibetan, and Chinese medicine, and now also rediscovered in the West.

The powers of the mind

Half a century ago Albert Einstein wrote, "a human being is part of the whole, called by us 'universe', a part limited in time and space. He experiences his thoughts and feelings as something separate from the rest — a kind of optical delusion of his consciousness. This delusion is a kind of prison for us, restricting us to our personal decisions and to affection for a few persons nearest us."

In our day the recognition of connectedness is returning to the natural sciences. Front-line investigators are leaving behind the classical views of matter and life. They perceive constant communication among all the things that co-exist and co-evolve in the biosphere. In this web of subtle and instantaneous communication and interaction human brains and minds are not excluded.

The new findings explode classical limits on the scope of human communication and interaction. In the classical view, also affirmed by common sense, connections that link people to each other and to their environment occur via the sensory organs: we see, hear, smell, touch, and taste the world beyond our body. It now appears — as the ancients and "primitives" have long known — that we are linked by more subtle connections as well. Leading-edge psychologists speak of such linkages as "transpersonal".

One strand of evidence for transpersonal connections comes from cultural anthropology. It appears that in their everyday life so-called primitive peoples make use of a closer form of communication among themselves than seeing, speaking, hearing, and touching. Medicine men and shamans appear to have the gift of clairvoyance and telepathy, elicited by a variety of techniques such as solitude, concentration, fasting, chanting, dancing, drumming, and ingesting psychedelic herbs. Entire tribes seem able to remain in touch with one another no matter where they roam, and can orient themselves in parts of their environment they have never seen. Anthropologists report that Australian aborigines can be informed of the fate of family and friends even when they are beyond the range of sensory communication with them. A man, far from his homeland, will announce that his father is dead, or his wife has given birth, or that there is some trouble in his country. He is so sure of his facts that he is ready to return home at once.

Among modern people spontaneous telepathy occurs mainly in identical twins and persons who are emotionally close to each other. "Twin pain" is a well-known phenomenon: one twin wakes up with a shock in the middle of the night just as the other suffers an accident, or feels a sudden pain in the leg accidentally hurt by the other. Spontaneous transpersonal connection among mothers and lovers is just as common: mothers seem often to know when their daughter is fending off an attacker, and wives when their husband is wounded or killed on the battlefield. These intuitions are frequent enough to convince a significant segment of the public.

Opinion surveys show that in 1996 belief in telepathy was shared by 56 per cent of the US population — up from 37 per cent in 1949 (reported in Newsweek, June 1996). Laboratory experiments themselves are rigorous enough also to convince a growing segment of the scientific community. A 1979 survey of 1,100 US college professors indicated that 55 per cent of natural scientists believed that telepathy, as other forms of ESP, is an established fact or a likely possibility, together with 66 per cent of the social scientists and 77 per cent of teachers in the humanities. Although at that time 34 per cent of the mainstream psychologists declared ESP an impossibility, only 3 per cent of the natural scientists were of this opinion, and none among the social scientists.

Further evidence of transpersonal links is furnished by history. Some form of extrasensory connection seems to have existed between entire groups of people — communities, cultures, whole civilizations: artifacts of striking similarity have been produced by cultures who have not even known of each other's existence.

In widely different locations archaic people developed an array of similar tools and artifacts. Giant pyramids have been built in distant locations with remarkable agreement in design: they were built in Ancient Egypt as well as in pre-Colombian America. Crafts, such as pottery-making, have taken much the same form in all cultures. The Acheulian hand axe, for example, a widespread tool of the Stone Age, had a typical almond or tear-shaped design chipped into symmetry on both sides. In Europe this axe was made of flint, in the Middle East of chert, and in Africa of quartzite, shale, or diabase. Its basic form was functional, yet the agreement in the details of its execution in virtually all traditional cultures cannot be explained by the simultaneous discovery of utilitarian solutions to a shared need: trial and error is not likely to have produced such similarity of detail in these many far-flung populations.

At the author's suggestion, University of Bologna historian Ignazio Masulli made an in-depth study of the pots, urns, and other artifacts produced by indigenous and independently evolving cultures in Europe, as well as Egypt, Persia, India, and China during the period from the 5th to the 2nd millennia BC. While he found striking recurrences in the basic forms and designs, he could not locate a conventional explanation for them. The civilizations were far apart in space and sometimes also in time, and did not seem to have had direct contact with each other.

The cultural-coincidence phenomenon is widespread. Although each culture added its own embellishments, Aztecs and Etruscans, Zulus and Malays, classical Indians and ancient Chinese built their monuments and fashioned their tools as if following a shared pattern or archetype. Certain archetypal symbols, such as Great Earth Mother, Hero's Journey, Mandala, Shadow, and Eternal Child have been recurring themes in the decorative and pictorial art of all times. They also appear in contemporary literature, drama, and cinema.

The laboratories of parapsychologists and the practices of psychotherapists are continually producing testable and repeatable evidence regarding transpersonal connections. Controlled tests on extrasensory perception (ESP) and other paranormal phenomena date from the 1930s, when J. B. Rhine conducted pioneering card- and dice-guessing experiments at Duke University. More recent experimental designs have become sophisticated, and experimental controls rigorous; physicists have often joined psychologists in carrying out the tests. A whole range of experimental protocols has been developed, from the noise-reduction technique known as the Ganzfeld technique to the highly respected DMILS (Direct Interaction with Living Systems) method. Explanations in terms of hidden sensory cues, machine bias, cheating by subjects, and experimenter incompetence or error have all been considered, but they were found unable to account for a number of statistically significant paranormal results. There appears to be an extremely subtle yet profound interconnection among living systems. In particular, human "senders" and "receivers" seem able to interact in ways that go beyond ordinary sense perception.

ESP experiments of modern scientific design began in the early 1970s, with Russell Targ's and Harold Puthoff's series of tests on thought and image transference. Targ and Puthoff placed the "receiver" in a sealed, opaque and electrically shielded chamber, and the "sender" in another room where he or she was subjected to bright flashes of light at regular intervals. The brain-wave patterns of both were registered on electro-encephalograph (EEG) machines. As expected, the sender exhibited the rhythmic brain waves that normally accompany exposure to bright flashes of light. However, after a brief interval the receiver also began to produce the same patterns, although he or she was not being directly exposed to the flashes, and was not receiving ordinary sense-perceivable signals from the sender.

Targ and Puthoff also conducted experiments on remote viewing. In these tests sender and receiver were separated by distances that precluded any form of sensory communication between them. At a site chosen at random, the sender acted as a "beacon"; the receiver then tried to pick up what the beacon saw. To document their impressions, receivers gave verbal descriptions, sometimes accompanied by sketches. Independent judges found the descriptions of the sketches matched the characteristics of the site that was actually seen by the beacon on average 66 per cent of the time.

More recently two physicists, Peter Stewart and Michael Brown in England, joined with Helen Stewart, a university administrator in New York, to test the reliability of a telepathic procedure "channeled" by Jane Roberts in her books on Seth. Transpersonal communication was attempted across the Atlantic in 14 accurately timed sessions between April and September 1994. Detailed records of the observations and impressions were made after each experience via E-mail, and they were stored on automatically dated and timed disks. Though the "clairvoyant" images were described in terms of associations rather than exact pictorial reproductions of the images seen by the sender, on the whole they corresponded to those images. The picture of a meteor shower, for example, came through as a snow-storm; the image of a tower with a rotating restaurant on top was picked up as a globe on a stand. Static images as well as dynamic sequences of images have been received — "still pictures" as well as "moving pictures".

Two occasions were particularly striking. On 5th September, Michael Brown, who expected Helen Stewart to be at her home in New York, picked up images of several Chinese model figures, of which one wore a red sarong and held a parasol. At first he was puzzled — until a reply from Helen clarified the image. It appears that at the time scheduled for the experiment Helen was sitting in a Chinese restaurant and from time to time her eyes drifted to dolls in the display windows. One of the dolls was dressed in a red and gold kimono and was holding a parasol. Helen was in a state of emotional charge and exhaustion, having just returned from the hospital where her daughter was being treated for an accident, and this may have contributed to the transmission of the image. On the second occasion Michael, in England, picked up an initial image that originated with Helen, who was then in Santa Fe. That image changed suddenly to a view through a window. Unknown at the time to Michael, at that precise instant Helen moved from one room to another and was looking out of a window in her new Santa Fe home. Reviewing the evidence collected in this series of tests, Peter Stewart concluded, "It is my view, as a scientist, that this demonstration fulfils the necessary criteria for scientific validation and accreditation of the Telepathic protocol and the experimental proof of the existence of the faculty."

Remote viewing experiments reported from other sources and laboratories involved various distances, ranging from half a mile to several thousand miles. Regardless of where they were carried out and by whom, the success rate was generally around 50 per cent — considerably above random probability. The most successful viewers were those who were relaxed, attentive, and meditative. They reported that they received a preliminary impression as a gentle and fleeting form which gradually evolved into an integrated image. They experienced the image as a surprise, both because it was clear and because it was clearly elsewhere.

Images, it appears, can also be transmitted while the receiver is asleep. Over a whole decade, Stanley Krippner and his associates carried out "dream ESP experiments" at the Dream Laboratory of Maimonides Hospital in New York City. The experiments followed a simple yet effective protocol. The volunteer, who would spend the night at the laboratory, would meet the sender and the experimenters on arrival and had the procedure explained to him or her. Electrodes were then affixed to the volunteer's head to monitor brain waves and eye movements; there was no further sensory contact with the sender until the next morning. One of the experimenters threw dice that, in combination with a random number table, gave a number corresponding to a sealed envelope containing an art print. The envelope was opened when the sender reached his or her room in a distant part of the hospital. Then he or she spent the night concentrating on the print.

The experimenters woke the subjects by intercom when the monitor indicated the end of a period of rapid eye-movement (REM) sleep. They were asked to describe any dream they might have had. The comments were recorded, together with the contents of an interview the next morning when the subjects were asked to associate with the remembered dreams. The interview was conducted double-blind — neither the subjects nor the experimenters knew which art print had been selected the night before.

Using data taken from the first night that each volunteer spent at the dream laboratory, the series of experiments between 1964 and 1969 produced 62 nights of data for analysis. They exhibited a significant correlation between the art print selected for a given night and the recipient's dreams on that night. The score was considerably higher on nights when there were few or no electrical storms in the area and sunspot activity was at a low ebb — when the Earth's geomagnetic field was relatively undisturbed.

Another example of transpersonal connection comes from the laboratory of Jacobo Grinberg-Zylberbaum at the National University of Mexico. In more than 50 experiments performed over five years, Grinberg-Zylberbaum paired his subjects inside sound- and electromagnetic radiation-proof "Faraday cages". He asked them to meditate together for 20 minutes, and then he placed them in separate Faraday cages where one subject was stimulated and the other not. The stimulated subject received stimuli at random intervals in such a way that neither he or she nor the experimenter knew when they were applied. The subjects who were not stimulated remained relaxed, with eyes closed, instructed to feel the presence of the partner without knowing anything about his or her stimulation.

In general, a series of one hundred stimuli were applied — such as flashes of light, sounds, or short, intense, but not painful electric shocks to the index and ring fingers of the right hand. The EEG of both subjects was then synchronized and examined for "normal" potentials evoked in the stimulated subject and "transferred" potentials in the non-stimulated person. Transferred potentials were not found in control situations without a stimulated subject, nor when a screen prevented the stimulated subject from perceiving the stimuli (such as light flashes), nor when the paired subjects did not previously interact. But during experimental situations with stimulated subjects and with interaction the transferred potentials appeared consistently in some 25 per cent of the cases. A particularly poignant example was furnished by a young couple, deeply in love. Their EEG patterns remained closely synchronized throughout the experiment, testifying that their report of feeling a deep oneness was not merely an illusion.

In a limited way, Grinberg-Zylberbaum could also replicate his results. When one individual exhibited the transferred potentials in one experiment, he or she usually exhibited them in subsequent experiments also. The results did not depend on spatial separation between senders and receivers — no matter how far or near they were to each other, the transfer effects remained the same.

Hundreds of experiments of this kind have now been carried out. They show that identifiable electrical signals occur with significant statistical frequency in the brain of one person, the "receiver," when a second person, the "sender," is meditating, given sensory stimulation, or is intentionally attempting to communicate. Signals occur even if senders and receivers are distant, and are sensorily and electromagnetically shielded.

One experiment this writer witnessed in person measured the degree of harmonization of the brain-waves of different subjects. In ordinary waking consciousness the two hemispheres of the brain — the language-oriented, linearly thinking rational "left brain", and the Gestalt-perceiving intuitive "right brain" — exhibit uncoordinated, randomly diverging wave patterns in the EEG. When a person enters a meditative state, these patterns tend to become synchronized, and in deep meditation the two hemispheres often fall into a nearly identical pattern. The experiment in question — carried out by physician and brain researcher Nitamo Montecucco in Milan and Rome — showed that in deep meditation not only the left and right brains of one and the same subject, also the left and right brains of different subjects manifest identical patterns. Tests with up to twelve meditating persons showed a close synchronization of the EEG waves of the entire group — even though there was no sensory contact among its members.

Physiological effects can be transmitted as well. Transmissions of this kind have come to be known as "telesomatic": they consist of physiological changes triggered in a targeted person by the mental processes of another. The pioneering study in this area is the work of cardiologist Randolph Byrd, a former professor at the University of California. His ten-month computer-assisted study concerned the medical histories of patients admitted to the coronary care unit at San Francisco General Hospital. Byrd formed a group of experimenters made up of ordinary people whose only common characteristic was a habit of regular prayer in Catholic or Protestant congregations around the country. The selected people were asked to pray for the recovery of a group of 192 patients; another set of 210 patients, for whom nobody prayed in the experiment, made up the control group. Rigid criteria were used: the selection was randomized and the experiment was carried out double-blind, with neither the patients, nor the nurses and doctors knowing which patients belonged to which group.

The experimenters were given the names of the patients, some information about their heart conditions, and were asked to pray for them every day. They were not told anything further. Since each experimenter could pray for several patients, each patient had between five and seven people praying for him or her. In terms of their probability statistics, the results were highly significant. The prayed-for group was five times less likely than the control group to require antibiotics (three versus 16 patients); it was three times less likely to develop pulmonary edema (six compared to 18 patients); none in the prayed-for group required endotracheal incubation (while 12 patients in the control group did); and fewer patients died in the former than in the latter group (though this particular result was statistically not significant). It did not matter how close or far the patients were to those who prayed for them, nor what type of praying was practiced. Only the fact of concentrated and repeated prayer seemed to have counted, without regard to whom the prayer was addressed and where it took place.

Such effects can also be transmitted in the form anthropologists call "sympathetic magic." It is known that shamans, witch doctors, and those who practice such magic — voodoo, for example — act not on the person they target, but on an effigy of that person, such as a doll.

The practice is widespread among traditional people; the rituals of Native Americans make use of it, too. In his famous study *The Golden Bough*, Sir James Frazer noted that practices among Native Americans include drawing the figure of a person in sand, ashes, or clay, and then pricking it with a sharp stick or doing it some other injury. The corresponding injury is said to beinflicted on the person the figure represents. Observers have found that a targeted person often falls ill, becomes lethargic, and sometimes even dies. Dean Radin and colleagues at the University of Nevada decided to test the positive variant of this effect under controlled laboratory conditions.

In Radin's experiments the subjects created a small doll in their own image, and included various small objects, pictures, jewelry, an autobiography, and personally meaningful tokens to "represent" them. They gave a list of what made them feel nurtured and comfortable. These and the accompanying information were used by the experimenter (the "healer", for the effects tested were beneficial rather than malign) to create a sympathetic connection to the "patient". The latter was wired up to monitor the activity of their autonomous nervous system — electrodermal activity, heart rate, blood pulse volume — while the healer was in an acoustically and electromagnetically shielded room in an adjacent building. The healer placed the doll and other small objects on the table in front of him and concentrated on them while sending randomly-sequenced "nurturing" (active healing) and "rest" messages.

It turned out that the electrodermal activity of the patients, together with their heart rate, were significantly different during the active nurturing periods than during the rest periods, while blood pulse volume was significant for a few seconds during the nurturing period. Both heart-rate and blood flow indicated a "relaxation response" — which made sense since the healer was attempting to "nurture" the subject via the doll. On the other hand, a higher rate of electrodermal activity showed that the patients' autonomic nervous systems were becoming aroused. This was puzzling, until the experimenters realized that the healers nurtured the patients by rubbing the shoulders of the dolls that represented them, or stroked their hair and face. This, apparently, had the effect of a "remote massage" on the patients.

Radin and colleagues concluded that the local actions and thoughts of the healer were mimicked in the remote patient almost as if healer and patient were next to each other. Distance between sender and receiver made little difference. This was confirmed in a large number of trials by experimental parapsychologists William Braud and Marilyn Schlitz regarding the impact of the mental imagery of senders on the physiology of receivers. Braud and Schlitz found that the mental images of the sender could reach out over space to cause changes in the physiology of a distant receiver; these effects are comparable to those one's own mental processes produce on one's body. "Telesomatic" action by a distant person appears nearly as effective as "psychosomatic" influence by the subjects themselves.

A considerable number of controlled studies demonstrate that some forms of psychic healing, from near or from far away, will augment the therapeutic effects of traditional medical treatments. In the US, an impressive number of controlled, double-blind studies on distant healing are being undertaken in medical schools and hospitals, and eleven eminent medical schools are now offering courses on the role of what they call spirituality in medical practice. In Britain, a recent study by psychiatrist Daniel Benor identified no less than 140 controlled trials of spiritual healing, of which 61 — or 44 per cent — had clearly documented therapeutic effects. Some researchers, notably US physician Larry Dossey, now speak of a new era in medical practice. Dossey calls it Era III, "nonlocal medicine". It follows Era II, mind-body medicine, and Era I, standard biochemical medicine.

Although pockets of scepticism remain, on the whole the debate in scientific circles has shifted from *whether* psychic healing effects occur to *how* they occur. There is no definitive answer yet, but the theories advanced by this writer, and the practical method developed among others by psychiatrist Lawrence LeShan, provide clues.[3] Using LeShan's method — which is teachable — the healer enters an altered state of consciousness, and this appears to prompt the patient to enter a similar state him- or herself. In an altered state self-healing powers seem to operate to better effect: the body's self-repair faculties are enhanced. This results in an improvement in the patient's condition — often enough to show up as a statistically significant healing effect.

A growing body of evidence indicates that altered states of consciousness (ASCs) have remarkable powers of information reception and communication.[3] These powers were known to all so-called "primitive" people who induced them by chanting, breathing, drumming, rhythmic dancing, fasting, social and sensory isolation, and even forms of physical pain. Some tribes, such as the !Kung Bushmen of the Kalahari desert, could all enter altered states at the same time. Semitic cultures used such states in the Cabalah, the Ancient Egyptians in the temple initiations of Isis and Osiris, and the classical Greeks in Bacchanalia and the rites of Attis and Adonis, as well as in the Eleusian mysteries. Native cultures of pre-Colombian America and Africa made use of them in shamanic procedures, healing ceremonies and rites of passage, and high-cultures of Asia applied them in various systems of yoga, Vipassana or Zen Buddhism, Tibetan Vajrayana, Taoism, and Sufism.

Until the advent of Western industrial civilization, most cultures held altered states in high esteem, for their powers of healing as well as their ability to mediate transpersonal contacts. But Western civilization has historically regarded most ASCs as pathological. It allows only dreaming sleep, dreamless sleep, daydreaming, alcolohic intoxication, and sexual orgasm as "normal" deviations from ordinary waking consciousness — all other ASCs have been condemned as signs of being either demented, or high on drugs. But the new "sciences of consciousness" adopt a less restrictive attitude. Here, work on altered states is becoming accepted as a legitimate area of scientific research.

Consciousness researcher and practicing psychiatrist John Nelson views ASCs as basic to the human psyche, with one end of the spectrum of its states shading into madness, and the other reaching to the loftiest realms of creativity, insight, and genius. But whether healthy or aberrant, regressive or transcendent, altered states share a significant characteristic: they make our connections to each other and to nature highly evident.

The altered-state interconnection of human consciousness with the world at large is of crucial importance for our times. It exhibits a fact that both mainstream science and mainstream public opinion has long disregarded: that our mind is spontaneously linked with other minds, and even with the cosmos as a whole. In this regard, Stanislav Grof's records of the verbal reports of his patients offer important evidence.

In almost 40 years of experience Grof transcribed the verbal reports of thousands of patients. Replacing psychedelic drugs with a non-invasive technique known as "holotropic breathing", Grof experienced no difficulty in inducing the required state in his patients. Once the altered state is attained, patients typically move back in their life, reliving earlier and earlier experiences and traumas — the Oedipus complex; toilet training; nursing; early infantile experience; the processes of biological birth. Reliving birth proves to be a particularly traumatic experience, involving profound existential and spiritual crisis, along with accompanying physical agony. Just at the point when patients feel that they are going irrevocably insane, and losing everything physically, psychologically, intellectually and spiritually, they report experiencing a dramatic expansion of horizons, and a radical change of perspective about the nature of reality. There is a sudden awakening, a feeling of being fundamentally connected to the universe. Experience of spiritual rebirth appears intertwined with experience of physical rebirth.

Grof's patients report a loosening and melting of the boundaries of the body ego, and a sense of merging with another person in unity and oneness. In some experiences they have a sense of complete identification to the point of losing awareness of their own identity. There is a further melting of ego boundaries in the experience of group identification and group consciousness. Rather than identifying with individual persons, individuals have a sense of becoming an entire group of people sharing some racial, cultural, national, ideological, political, or professional characteristics. The depth, scope, and intensity of this experience can reach extraordinary proportions: people experience the totality of suffering of all the soldiers who have ever died on the battlefield since the beginning of history, the desire of revolutionaries of all ages to overthrow a tyrant, or the love, tenderness, and dedication of all mothers in regard to their babies. Identification can focus on a social or political group, the people of an entire country or continent, all members of a race, or all followers of a religion.

Individuals can also achieve a realistic identification with various species of animals. The experience is authentic and convincing, including body image; specific physiological sensations; instinctual drives; unique perceptions of the environment, and the corresponding emotional reactions. In a still more embracing experience patients expand their consciousness to such an extent that it encompasses the totality of life on this planet, including all of humanity and all the flora and fauna of the biosphere. Experiences can also penetrate beyond the sphere of life, to the macroscopic and microscopic phenomena of the inorganic world. Patients report experiential identification with the waters of rivers and oceans, with various forms of fire, with the Earth and with mountains, and with the forces unleashed in natural catastrophes such as electric storms, earthquakes, tornadoes, and volcanic eruptions. Grof concluded that every process in the universe that can be objectively observed in the ordinary state of consciousness can be subjectively experienced in the altered state.

Altered-state experiences bridge displacements in time. Subjects may not only recall their intra-uterine experiences as a fetus, but can also have historically verifiable racial experiences and the experience of past lives. The essential characteristic of the latter is a convinced sense of remembering something that had already happened to them, but not in the present lifetime. Subjects maintain their sense of individuality and personal identity, but experience themselves in another form, at another place and time, and in another context. In these "reincarnation-type experiences" the birth of the individual is a point of transformation, where the enduring record of multiple lifetimes enters the present lifetime.

Based on evidence gathered in nearly four decades of analysis, Grof came to the view that the human psyche has unexpected dimensions. In addition to the "biographic-recollective" domain of ordinary-state consciousness and memory, the psyche possesses "perinatal" and "transpersonal" domains. The perinatal domain conveys experiences that occurred before the birth of the individual; while the transpersonal domain mediates connection between the mind and practically any part or aspect of the universe.

Vaçlav Havel wrote that we seem to have an antenna in our head that picks up signals from a transmitter that contains the experience of the entire human race. The experiences of scores of transpersonal psychologists and consciousness researchers bears out this intuition. It indicates that in altered states of consciousness we can access the thoughts, images, and feelings of hosts of other persons, even the "feel" of animals and inanimate objects.

The evidence that surfaces, surprising as it may be, indicates that our brain is not limited to the neural processes that go on in within our cranium — it is a wide-band receiver and high-powered processor of information. The information it receives originates not only in our own body, but comes from all over the world. The brain's ten billion neurons, with 10,000 connections each, constitute the most complex system of electronic organization in the known universe. This system, which operates at the edge of chaos, receives and transforms information from our own body, as well as the electromagnetic, acoustic, and other wave fields in our environment. It also receives and decodes information from more subtle fields, including the vacuum's zero-point holofield. Potentially, our brain connects us with the wide reaches of the cosmos.

As mystics, prophets, and people of insight and sensitivity intuited through the ages, our brain is an integral part of the universe, and our mind is a potentially open window on it. It is up to us to throw open that window, to the full extent of our remarkable, but hitherto largely unexploited, physical and mental capacities.

The insights into the nature of matter, life, and mind conveyed by the new sciences are crucial for our times. The findings speak of a cosmos in continuous if subtle intercommunication — a "whispering pond" — in which human beings are not strangers but integral parts. More than that: as conscious parts capable of knowing and planning their actions, humans are key participants in the evolution of this subtle cosmic pond as it unfolds on our small but richly endowed planet.

This should give us a new sense of significance, and also a deep sense of responsibility. We may be inhabitants of a small planet on a smallish solar system at the edge of a galaxy, but surely we, with our conscious mind, are one of the highly evolved manifestations of the great trend that brought forth galaxies, stars and planets in cosmic spacetime, and created life of ever more complex form on the surface of sun-bathed planets. Given our place and role in the grand scheme of things it is our cosmic responsibility to tread a positive path to development — to find our way to a world where individuality, innovation, and diversity are not the source of disunity, conflict, and degradation, but the basis for harmony, cooperation, and coevolution.

[1] see Ervin Laszlo, *The Interconnected Universe,* World Scientific, Singapore and London, 1994.

[2] I am grateful to David Loye for calling this passage to my attention.

[3] Further details are in Ervin Laszlo, *The Whispering Pond: A Personal Guide to the Emerging Vision of Science*, Element Books, Shaftesbury and Rockport, 1996.

THE CLUB OF BUDAPEST

The Club of Budapest was founded at the end of 1993 in recognition of the urgent need to evolve a new consciousness. An informal association of leading artists, writers, spiritual persons, and creative individuals from all spheres, the Club focuses the creativity embodied in its Members to provide meaningful examples of the new consciousness, and to catalyze it in the minds of decision-makers and the general public. To this end the Club is undertaking a number of projects. Its mission statement spells out the philosophy that underlies them.

"At the turn of the 21st century we live in an epoch of transition; witnessing the deepest and fastest transformation in the history of humanity. This transformation is not without crises and difficulties, the birthpangs of a coming age. Today hundreds of millions are without work; one thousand million or more are exploited by poor wages; three thousand million are forced into growing poverty. On the one hand the population of the world is growing, on the other the number of jobs is diminishing. The gap between rich and poor economies, and between rich and poor people within nations, is increasing. The problems of the environment, as those of society, confront all people (....)"

"The ecological problem, the employment problem, the developmental problem, the population problem, the armaments problem, and the many problems of energies and resources will not be overcome merely by reducing the number of already useless nuclear warheads, nor by signing politically softened treaties on world trade, dangerous technologies, global warming, biological diversity, and sustainable development. More is required today than piecemeal action and short-term problem-solving. The fact is that, as Einstein remarked, one cannot solve a problem with the same kind of thinking that gave rise to that problem. The approaching crises we face are due to ways of thinking that lag behind the needs of the times; the crucial factor in coping with them is an updated and upgraded way of thinking — and feeling — in today's societies."

"Updating and upgrading today's ways of thinking and feeling is a challenging task, but not an intractable one. The required concepts are largely known, the indicated technologies and practices are for the most part already developed. The missing factor is the commitment of people young and old to the indicated objectives, and their willingness to adopt the corresponding practices. If this hiatus is to be filled, more is required than intellectual understanding alone. Intellectual understanding must be undergirded by empathy and intuition, by fresh values and a new commitment. When all is said and done, we come to a basic insight: we need a more evolved consciousness. Entering the 21st century with the consciousness that hallmarked the 20th century would be like entering the modern age with the consciousness of the Middle Ages. It would be not only inappropriate, but dangerous."

The Club of Budapest, and its Members, coordinators, friends, and associates are dedicated to the proposition that promoting and facilitating the evolution of a new consciousness is vital for our individual and collective wellbeing, and the future of all life on this planet.

THE MAJOR PROJECTS

The required shift in today's ways of thinking calls for fresh sensitivity, deeper insights, and more timely values: precisely the resources that great writers, artists, scientists, and spiritually oriented people have always brought to their times. The global projects of The Club of Budapest are designed to re-vitalize, concentrate, and empower these vital, but as yet vastly underutilized, sources of human and social creativity. To this end the Presidium of the Club adopted, and implements jointly with its Members, Ambassadors, Trustees, National Associations and Regional Centers, international and intercultural projects to highlight, motivate, and facilitate the emergence of a more involved consciousness in individuals, communities, public institutions, as well as business enterprises.

Projects currently adopted fall into four general categories:

• projects that draw on scientific knowledge joined with artistic, literary, and spiritual insight to identify responsible ways of thinking and acting, with particular attention to the requirements of elementary, middle-level, professional, and higher education;

• projects that communicate the necessary insights through the electronic and the printed media;

• projects that help business organizations to achieve a globally effective and ethically responsible standard of thinking and acting in their own spheres of activity;

• consulting services aimed at selecting, endorsing, and facilitating the acceptance of products and services that meet the standards of globally conscious and responsible ethics.

The Club's international and intercultural projects are complemented by in-depth consultations at the annual Members' Meetings.

THE SCIENCE, ART, AND EDUCATION-RELATED PROJECTS

The Manifesto on the Spirit of Planetary Consciousness

Drafted in consultation with the Dalai Lama, Tsingis Aitmatov, Peter Ustinov, Vigdis Finnbogadóttir, Edgar Mitchell, Peter Russell, Betty Williams, Elie Wiesel and other Honorary Members, the Manifesto highlights the responsibility of today's people, enterprises, and governments for entering on a path toward humane and sustainable evolution. Signed and proclaimed by the Dalai Lama and the other signatories in an international media event held in Budapest on 27th October 1996, the Manifesto is now disseminated internationally on the electronic as well as the printed media. (The full text of the Manifesto is reproduced after this Annex.)

The Planetary Consciousness Prize

The Planetary Consciousness Prize of The Club of Budapest is awarded annually to individuals who have exhibited a highly evolved consciousness and have made an outstanding contribution to its spread in society. The Planetary Consciousness World Leadership Prize honors a personality whose thinking and consciousness have made, and continue to make, a significant impact on world affairs. The Planetary Consciousness World Innovation Prize, in turn, is awarded to an individual whose artistic, literary, political, or business activity has demonstrated the new consciousness in an innovative and effective manner. The Planetary Consciousness World Media Prize is awarded to a media personality whose activities have made a crucial contribution to the communication of the new consciousness through the electronic or printed media. The Prizes are presented by the Club's Honorary Members in the major capitals and cultural centers of the world.

The 1996 World Leadership Prize was awarded to Czech writer -president Vaçlav Havel, and the Innovation Prize was shared by Hungarian folk-dance and music researchers and activitists Sándor Timár, Béla Halmos, and Ferene Sebő. They were presented by Lord Yehudi Menuhin and Sir Peter Ustinov in the framework of a concert conducted by Ken-ichiro Kobayashi on 26th October 1996 in the city of Budapest.

The 1997 Leadership Prize was awarded to political thinker and former Soviet President Mikhail Gorbachev, and the Innovation Prize was shared by Grameen Bank President and microcredit innovator Mohammed Yunus, and Terra Project initiator and creative entrepreneur Huschmand Sabet, presented on 25th June 1997 in the city of Frankfurt am Main.

The World Media Prize will be awarded for the first time in March 1998, in a special gala event in the framework of the Prince Award Ceremonies in the city of Budapest.

"The Chances of Evolution": World Evolutionary Thinkers Symposium and Dialogues, Weimar, 1999

Following a period of intensive research and discussion (1997–1998), 24 leading-edge scientists, members and associates of the General Evolution Research Group, with competence in fields ranging from cosmology to psychology, through biology and the human and social sciences, will report on the long-term chances of evolution for humanity on this planet. The Report will be shared by scientists as well as the general public in the framework of the cultural events celebrating "Weimar: Cultural Capital of Europe 1999". In order that the conclusions and recommendations of the Report may penetrate a wide segment of contemporary society, a series of dialogs with leading-edge artists, writers, and other creative individuals will be organized throughout the year 1999. Out of these encounters meaningful guidelines are expected to emerge which will promote effective and responsible thinking and acting — compass points for satisfying the conditions under which individuals and societies can evolve in a sustainable and humane manner in the next century.

Educational Implications of "The Chances of Evolution": World Evolutionary Thinkers Symposium and Dialogues

The scientists' Report and the ensuing dialogs on the long-term chances of evolution for humanity promise to be of particular significance for young people of the next generations, who will enjoy, or else suffer, the consequences of the decisions and actions of the present generation. The Club of Budapest intends to join forces with UNESCO and other globally oriented educational organizations to develop educational materials incorporating essential elements of the Report, and its elaboration through artists, writers, and other creative individuals, in a form suitable for elementary, middle, and professional schools, as well as for universities and other institutions of continuing and higher education.

The Graduate Institute of Planetary Consciousness Studies
Headquarters at the Monterrey Institute of Technology at Guanajuato, Mexico

While the evolution of human consciousness has been ongoing since the dawn of civilization, the ability consciously to affect the evolution of humanity is a new and as yet unexploited capacity. As this Report noted, developing this capacity and putting it to work calls for further evolving our consciousness to embrace the problems, and the potentials, of today's complex and globalized world.

Genuine literacy in the contemporary world calls for combining expertise in a specialized sphere of investigation with familiarity with a broad range of current issues. In the case of Planetary Consciousness Studies, the specialized area of expertise is the nature and evolution of human consciousness; the broad area of investigation concerns today's characteristic trends and processes. Courses and seminars to be offered include:

• The Role of Individual and Collective Consciousness at the Turn of the 21st Century

• Evolving Consciousness for Conscious Evolution: the Past, Present, and Future of Social Evolution

• The Evolution of Human Consciousness: Past Developments and Prospects for the Future

• Planetary Consciousness Ethics

• Practical Systems Design for the Evolution of Planetary Consciousness

"Peace-Building through Culture": A Series of Networked Activities by the Club's Regional Centers

Complementing projects designed at the Club's headquarters, the members of the Regional Centers for Planetary Consciousness undertake a series of locally designed and autonomously implemented activities. The projects share an overall focus: the power and potential of the arts, literature, and the spiritual domains to create empathy and achieve solidarity among people, both within and between cultures. Proposed and advised by the West Coast Regional Center (San Francisco), the diverse activities are networked through the Internet and coordinated by the Club's international secretariat in London.

THE MEDIA-RELATED PROJECTS

The Evolutionary Responsibility World Media Forum, Costa Rica 1999

Given that the public's perceptions, valuations, and thinking determine the level of support needed to implement effective and responsible governmental policies, corporate strategies and grassroots initiatives, the role of the media is a critical determinant of our common future. The Media Forum will discuss responsible editorial policy and programming as a support for the evolution of the new consciousness throughout today's populations. Prepared in collaboration with the Seminars on Peace Journalism, as well as through a series of workshops beginning in February 1998, the event organized in the framework of the UN University for Peace in Costa Rica will offer a forum for informal debate and dialog for the world's media leaders and thinkers.

"The Universal Couch" Planetary Consciousness Portraits of the Turn of the Century

People worldwide express themselves in in-depth interviews on subjects such as tolerance, solidarity, work, and the future, giving insight into their own personal values, fears, and expectations. In the series of TV portraits under the auspices of The Club of Budapest, Horst Wackerbarth and Club Vice President Thomas Druyen will carry out some 50,000 interviews with leading figures, public heroes, megastars, significant personalities from diverse walks of life, as well as children and ordinary people from many countries. This documentation of the state of human consciousness at the turn of the century will be recorded on television and communicated through photographs, films, video-clips, TV, magazines, books, exhibitions, and the Internet. A special series focuses on the theme "planetary consciousness," documenting varied aspects and dimensions of the new ways of thinking, feeling, and perceiving.

Seminars on "Peace Journalism"

Offered in collaboration with the International Peace College of Berlin, the Seminars are aimed at leading, as well as young and promising, journalists. They are conducted by authorities in the field of journalism and public affairs, and will look at the form, content, and marketing of reports on events and activities which concern disarmament, the peaceful resolution of conflicts, and peace-making actions and projects in general. The emphasis is on a spirit of responsibility in reporting on wars and conflict situations, with particular attention to questions such as:

• how can a special profession of "peace journalists" be formed?

• how can a market be created for the reports of peace journalists?

• how are media moguls, editors, and producers to be convinced of the need for developing such a market?

• on what aspects of a situation should peace journalists focus their attention?

• what should constitute the principal elements of a basic code of peace journalism?

• how can peace journalists be trained for their job?

THE BUSINESS-RELATED PROJECTS AND CONSULTING SERVICES

Initiating and Guiding Responsible Policy in Individual Corporations

Teams of experts appointed by the Club are to be available to enterprises and other organizations which wish to ensure that their policies and strategies meet the standard for a new and timely corporate culture. The teams will work with organizations and enterprises to research the match between institutional or company structure, production processes and service offerings, and the standards of socially and environmentally responsible behavior. Remedial actions will be recommended as necessary, and their implementation supervised. Positively evaluated structures, products and processes will be endorsed and their example disseminated among the public. The entire process is to be exhaustively documented and evaluated.

Convening and Servicing Total Responsibility Councils (TRCs)

TRCs are The Club of Budapest's forum for market leaders who wish to adopt socially and environmentally responsible corporate policies, and wish to join forces in order to seize jointly attainable opportunities and share the corresponding costs. The partnerships forged are expected to work toward creating codes of conduct for industry, so as to avert short-term opportunism by unscrupulous competitors and potential free-riders. The Club offers ongoing consulting and advisory, as well as logistical support services for the meetings of the Councils, and for monitoring the effective implementation of their self-regulatory codes and related decisions.

MEMBERS' MEETINGS

The Club brings together its Members for general discussion and consultation once each year. The 1996 Meeting took place at the Budapest Headquarters from 12th to 15th May 1996. The 1997 Meeting is in cooperation with the Université Interdisciplinaire de Paris on 5th and 6th December 1997 at UNESCO headquarters in Paris, while the 1998 Meeting is scheduled for the city of Strasbourg in cooperation with Strasbourg Promotion Evénement and The Council of Europe.

PUBLICATIONS

Reinforcing and documenting the Club's international and inter-cultural projects, the series of publications initiated by The Club of Budapest provides guidelines for new thinking and action in the context of the changing parameters of the current economic, social, human, and ecological situation. Published materials are oriented to fill the need for meaningful information by the general public, the need for forward-looking materials in the educational system, and the corresponding need for compass points for ethical and responsible leadership by decision-makers in business and politics. Brief notes and notices are published in the Club's Viewsletter and on its Web homepage; articles and research reports in the international quarterly World Futures: The Journal of General Evolution (Gordon & Breach publishers, Amsterdam), and full-length monographs and collections of studies in the associated General Evolution Studies book series.

Club of Budapest Web address:
http://newciv.org/ClubofBudapest

MANIFESTO ON THE SPIRIT OF PLANETARY CONSCIOUSNESS

The new requirements of thought and action

1. In the closing years of the 20th century, we have reached a crucial juncture in our history. We are on the threshold of a new stage of social, spiritual and cultural evolution, a stage that is as different from the stage of the earlier decades of this century as the grasslands were from the caves, and settled villages from life in nomadic tribes. We are evolving out of the nationally based industrial societies that were created at the dawn of the first industrial revolution, and heading toward an interconnected, information-based social, economic, and cultural system that straddles the globe. The path of this evolution is not smooth: it is filled with shocks and surprises. This century has witnessed several major shock waves, and others may come our way before long. The way we shall cope with present and future shocks will decide our future, and the future of our children and grandchildren.

2. The challenge we now face is the challenge of choosing our destiny. Our generation, of all the thousands of generations before us, is called upon to decide the fate of life on this planet. The processes we have initiated within our lifetime and the lifetime of our fathers and grandfathers cannot continue in the lifetime of our children and grandchildren. Whatever we do either creates the framework for reaching a peaceful and cooperative global society and thus continuing the grand adventure of life, spirit, and consciousness on Earth, or sets the stage for the termination of humanity's tenure on this planet.

3. The patterns of action in today's world are not encouraging. Millions of people are without work; millions are exploited by poor wages; millions are forced into helplessness and poverty. The gap between rich and poor nations, and between rich and poor people within nations, is great and still growing. Though the world community is relieved of the specter of superpower confrontation and is threatened by ecological collapse, the world's governments still spend a thousand billion dollars a year on arms and the military and only a tiny fraction of this sum on maintaining a livable environment.

4. The militarization problem, the developmental problem, the ecological problem, the population problem, and the many problems of energy and raw materials will not be overcome merely by reducing the number of already useless nuclear warheads, nor by signing politically softened treaties on world trade, global warming, biological diversity, and sustainable development. More is required today than piecemeal action and short-term problem-solving. We need to perceive the problems in their complex totality, and grasp them not only with our reason and intellect, but with all the faculties of our insight and empathy. Beyond the powers of the rational mind, the remarkable faculties of the human spirit embrace the power of love, of compassion, and of solidarity. We must not fail to call upon their remarkable powers when confronting the task of initiating the embracing, multi-faceted approaches that alone could enable us to reach the next stage in the evolution of our sophisticated but unstable and vulnerable socio-technological communities.

5. If we maintain obsolete values and beliefs, a fragmented consciousness and a self-centered spirit, we also maintain outdated goals and behaviors. And such behaviors by a large number of people would block the entire transition to an interdependent yet peaceful and cooperative global society. There is now both a moral and a practical obligation for each of us to look beyond the surface of events, beyond the plots and polemics of practical policies, the sensationalistic headlines of the mass media, and the fads and fashions of changing lifestyles and styles of work — an obligation to feel the ground swell underneath the events and perceive the direction they are taking: to evolve the spirit and the consciousness that could enable us to perceive the problems and the opportunities — and to act on them.

A call for creativity and diversity

6. A new way of thinking has become the necessary condition for responsible living and acting. Evolving it means fostering creativity in all people, in all parts of the world. Creativity is not a genetic but a cultural endowment of human beings. Culture and society change fast, while genes change slowly: no more than one half of one percent of the human genetic endowment is likely to alter in an entire century. Hence most of our genes date from the Stone Age or before; they could help us to live in the jungles of nature but not in the jungles of civilization. Today's economic, social, and technological environment is our own creation, and only the creativity of our mind — our culture, spirit and consciousness — could enable us to cope with it. Genuine creativity does not remain paralyzed when faced with unusual and unexpected problems but confronts them openly, without prejudice. Cultivating it is a precondition of finding our way toward a globally interconnected society in which individuals, enterprises, states, and the whole family of peoples and nations could live together peacefully, cooperatively, and with mutual benefit.

7. Sustained diversity is another requirement of our age. Diversity is basic to all things in nature and in art: a symphony cannot be made of one tone or even played by one instrument; a painting must have many shapes and perhaps many colors; a garden is more beautiful if it contains flowers and plants of many different kinds. A multicellular organism cannot survive if it is reduced to one kind of cell; even sponges evolve cells with specialized functions. And more complex organisms have cells and organs of a great variety, with a great variety of mutually complementary and exquisitely co-ordinated functions. Cultural and spiritual diversity in the human world is just as essential as diversity in nature and in art. A human community must have members that are different from one another not only in age and sex; but also in personality, color, and creed. Only then could its members perform the tasks that each does best, and complement each other so that the whole formed by them could grow and evolve. The evolving global society would have great diversity, were it not for the unwanted and undesirable uniformity introduced through the domination of a handful of cultures and societies. Just as the diversity of nature is threatened by cultivating only one or a few varieties of crops and husbanding only a handful of species of animals, so the diversity of today's world is endangered by the domination of one, or at the most a few, varieties of cultures and civilizations.

8. The world of the 21st century will be viable only if it maintains essential elements of the diversity that has always hallmarked cultures, creeds, economic, social and political orders as well as of ways of life. Sustaining diversity does not mean isolating peoples and cultures from one another: it calls for international and inter-cultural contact and communication with due respect for each other's differences, beliefs, lifestyles, and ambitions. Sustaining diversity also does not mean preserving inequality, for equality does not reside in uniformity, but in the recognition of the equal value and dignity of all peoples and cultures. Creating a diverse yet equitable and intercommunicating world calls for more than just paying lip-service to equality and just tolerating each other's differ-ences. Letting others be what they want as long as they stay in their corner of the world, and letting them do what they want "as long as they don't do it in my backyard" are well-meaning but inadequate attitudes. As the diverse organs in a body, diverse peoples and cultures need to work together to maintain the whole system in which they are a part, a system that is the human community in its planetary abode. In the last decade of the 20th century, different nations and cultures must develop the compassion and the solidarity that could enable all of us to go beyond the stance of passive tolerance, to actively work with and complement each other.

A call for responsibility

9. In the course of the 20th century, people in many parts of the world have become conscious of their rights as well as of many persistent violations of them. This development is important, but in itself it is not enough. In the remaining years of this century we must also become conscious of the factor without which neither rights nor other values can be effectively safeguarded: our individual and collective responsibilities. We are not likely to grow into a peaceful and cooperative human family unless we become responsible social, economic, political, and cultural actors.

10. We human beings need more than food, water, and shelter; more even than remunerated work, self-esteem, and social acceptance. We also need something to live for: an ideal to achieve, a responsibility to accept. Since we are aware of the consequences of our actions, we can and must accept responsibility for them. Such responsibility goes deeper than many of us may think. In today's world all people, no matter where they live and what they do, have become responsible for their actions as:
  • private individuals;
  • citizens of a country;
  • collaborators in business and the economy;
  • member of the human community;
  • persons endowed with mind and consciousness.

As individuals, we are responsible for seeking our interests in harmony with, and not at the expense of, the interests and well-being of others; responsible for condemning and averting any form of killing and brutality, responsible for not bringing more children into the world than we truly need and can support, and for respecting the right to life, development, and equal status and dignity of all the children, women, and men who inhabit the Earth.

As citizens of our country, we are responsible for demanding that our leaders beat swords into ploughshares and relate to other nations peacefully and in a spirit of cooperation; that they recognize the legitimate aspirations of all communities in the human family; and that they do not abuse sovereign powers to manipulate people and the environment for shortsighted and selfish ends.

As collaborators in business and actors in the economy, we are responsible for ensuring that corporate objectives do not center uniquely on profit and growth, but include a concern that products and services respond to human needs and demands without harming people and impairing nature; that they do not serve destructive ends and unscrupulous designs; and that they respect the rights of all enterpreneurs and enterprises who compete fairly in the global marketplace.

As members of the human community, it is our responsibility to adopt a culture of non-violence, solidarity, and economic, political and social equality, promoting mutual understanding and respect among people and nations whether they are like us or different, demanding that all people everywhere should be empowered to respond to the challenges that face them with the material as well as spiritual resources that are required for this unprecedented task.

And as persons endowed with mind and consciousness, our responsibility is to encourage comprehension and appreciation for the excellence of the human spirit in all its manifestations, and for inspiring awe and wonder for a cosmos that brought forth life and consciousness and holds out the possibility of its continued evolution toward ever higher levels of insight, understanding, love, and compassion.

A call for planetary consciousness

11. In most parts of the world, the real potential of human beings is sadly underdeveloped. The way children are raised depresses their faculties for learning and creativity; the way young people experience the struggle for material survival results in frustration and resentment. In adults this leads to a variety of compensatory, addictive, and compulsive behaviors. The result is the persistence of social and political oppression, economic warfare, cultural intolerance, crime, and disregard for the environment. Eliminating social and economic ills and frustrations calls for considerable socio-economic development, and that is not possible without better education, information, and communication. These, however, are blocked by the absence of socio-economic development, so that a vicious cycle is produced: underdevelopment creates frustration, and frustration, giving rise to defective behaviors, blocks development. This cycle must be broken at its point of greatest flexibility, and that is the development of the spirit and consciousness of human beings. Achieving this objective does not preempt the need for socio-economic development with all its financial and technical resources, but calls for a parallel mission in the spiritual field. Unless people's spirit and consciousness evolves to the planetary dimension, the processes that stress the globalized society/nature system will intensify and create a shock wave that could jeopardize the entire transition toward a peaceful and cooperative global society. This would be a setback for humanity and a danger for everyone. Evolving human spirit and consciousness is the first vital cause shared by the whole of the human family.

12. In our world static stability is an illusion, the only permanence is in sustainable change and transformation. There is a constant need to guide the evolution of our societies so as to avoid breakdowns and progress toward a world where all people can live in peace, freedom, and dignity. Such guidance does not come from teachers and schools, not even from political and business leaders, though their commitment and role are important. Essentially and crucially, it comes from each person himself and herself. An individual endowed with planetary consciousness recognizes his or her role in the evolutionary process and acts responsibly in light of this perception. Each of us must start with himself or herself to evolve his or her consciousness to this planetary dimension; only then can we become responsible and effective agents of our society's change and transformation. Planetary consciousness is the knowing as well as the feeling of the vital interdependence and essential oneness of humankind, and the conscious adoption of the ethics and the ethos that this entails. Its evolution is the basic imperative of human survival on this planet.

A BIBLIOGRAPHY OF THE SCIENTIFIC FINDINGS QUOTED IN THIS REPORT

Artigiani, Robert, *Changing Visions: Human Cognitive Maps Past, Present, and Future*, in Ervin Laszlo, Robert Artigiani, Allan Combs, and Vilmos Csányi, Adamantine Press, London, 1996

Benor, Daniel J, *Healing Research Vol. 1*, Helix Editions, London, 1993

——, *Healing Research: Holistic Energy Medicine and Spiritual Healing*, Helix Verlag, Munich,1993

——, "Survey of spiritual healing research," Contemporary Medical Research, Vol. 4, 9 (1990)

Bohm, David, *Wholeness and the Implicate Order*, Routledge & Kegan Paul, London, 1980

Braud, W. and M. Schlitz, "Psychokinetic influence on electrodermal activity," Journal of Parapsychology, Vol. 47 (1983)

Capra, Fritzhof, *The Web of Life*, Anchor Books, New York, 1996

Celente, Gerald, "Global Simplicity," The Trends Journal, Vol. VI, 1, Winter 1997

Commission on Global Governance, *Our Global Neighborhood*, Oxford University Press, New York, 1995

Crick, Francis, *The Astonishing Hypothesis*, Charles Scribner, New York, 1994

Cyber: "Ricerche Olistiche (Nitamo Montecucco)," in Cyber (Milan), November 1992

Davies, Paul, *God and the New Physics*, Simon & Schuster, New York, 1983

——, and John Gribbin, *The Matter Myth*, Simon & Schuster, New York, 1992

——, *The Mind of God*, Simon & Schuster, New York, 1992

Del Giudice, E., G., S. Doglia, M. Milani, and G. Vitiello, in F. Guttmann and H. Keyzer (eds), *Modern Bioelectrochemistry*, Plenum, New York, 1986

Diamond, Jared, "Easter's End", Discover, Vol. 168, 1995

Dossey, Larry, *Recovering the Soul: A Scientific and Spiritual Search*, New York, Bantam, 1989
——, *Healing Words: The Power of Prayer and the Practice of Medicine*, Harper, San Francisco, 1993
Elgin, Duane, *Global Consciousness Change: Indicators of an Emerging Paradigm*, Millennium Project, San Anselmo, CA, 1997
——, *Awakening Earth: Exploring the Evolution of Human Culture and Consciousness*, Morrow, New York, 1993
Environmental Monitor, Health and Planet Survey of International Environment Monitor Ltd (IEML) Ottawa, Canada, 1997
Feinstein, David, "At play in fields of the mind: Personal myths as fields of information", Journal of Humanistic Psychology, 1997
——, and Stanley Krippner, *The Mythic Path*, Tarcher Putnam, New York, 1997
Freeman, W.J. and J.M.Barrie, "Chaotic oscillations and the genesis of meaning in cerebral cortex." in *Temporal Coding in the Brain*, ed. G. Bizsaki, Springer Verlag, Berlin, 1994
Fröhlich, H. "Long range coherence and energy storage in biological systems." Int. Journal of Quantum Chemistry 2, 1980
——, (ed.) *Biological Coherence and Response to External Stimuli*, Springer Verlag, Heidelberg, 1988
Gazdag, László, "Superfluid mediums, vacuum spaces" Speculations in Science and Technology, Vol. 12,1, 1989
——, "Combining of the gravitational and electromagnetic fields," ibid., Vol. 16,1, 1993
Goodwin, Brian, "Development and evolution," Journal of Theoretical Biology, 97, 1982
——, "Organisms and minds as organic forms," Leonardo, 22, 1, 1989
Gore, Al, *Earth in the Balance*, Houghton Mifflin, Boston, 1992
Grinberg-Zylverbaum, Jacobo M. Delaflor, M.E. Sanchez-Arellano, M.A. Guevara, and M. Perez, "Human communication and the electrophysiological activity of the brain" Subtle Energies, Vol. 3,3, 1993
Grof, Stanislav, *The Adventure of Self-discovery*, State University of New York Press, Albany, 1988
——, *Beyond the Brain*, State University of New York Press, Albany, 1985
——, with Hal Zina Bennett, *The Holotropic Mind*, Harper, San Francisco, 1993
Grosso, Michael, *The Millennium Myth: Love and Death at the End of*

Time, Quest, Wheaton, IL, 1995

Haisch, Bernhard and Alfonso Rueda, and H.E. Puthoff, "Inertia as a zero-point-field Lorentz force," Physical Review A, 49.2, February 1994

Hansen, G.M., M. Schlitz and C. Tart, "Summary of remote viewing research," in Russell Targ and K. Harary, *The Mind Race, 1972-1982,* Villard, New York, 1984

Ho, Mae Wan, *The Rainbow and the Worm: The Physics of Organisms,* World Scientific, Singapore and London, 1993

——, "Bioenergetics, biocommunication and organic space-time," in *Living Computers,* ed. A.M. Fedorec and P.J. Marcer, The University of Greenwich, 1996

——, and Peter Saunders, "Liquid crystalline mesophases in living organisms." in *Bioelectromagnetism and Biocommunication,* ed. Mae Wan Ho, F.A. Popp and U. Warnke, World Scientific, Singapore and London, 1994

Honorton, C. R. Berger, M. Varvoglis, M. Quant, P. Derr, E. Schechter, and D. Ferrari, "Psi-communication in the Ganzfeld: Experiments with an automated testing system and a comparison with a meta-analysis of earlier studies." Journal of Parapsychology, 54, 1990

Hoyle, Fred, *The Intelligent Universe,* Michael Joseph, 1983

Human Development Report 1996, United Nations Development Programme, Mahbub ul Haq and Richard Jolly, principal coordinators, Oxford University Press, New York, 1996

Jung, Carl G., *The Collected Works of C.G. Jung,* Princeton University Press, Princeton, NJ 1958, vol. 8, para. 417

Keen, Sam, *Hymns to an Unknown God,* Bantam, New York, 1994

Laszlo, Ervin, *The Creative Cosmos,* see following Selected Bibliography

——, *The Interconnected Universe,* see below

——, *The Choice: Evolution or Extinction,* see below

——, *The Whispering Pond,* see below

——, *Evolution: The General Theory,* see below

——, *The Systems View of the World,* see below

——, and Christopher Laszlo, *The Insight Edge: An Introduction to the Theory and Practice of Evolutionary Management,* see below

Morin, Edgar and Anne Brigitte Kern, *Terre-Patrie,* Editions du Seuil, Paris 1993.

Nelson, John E, *Healing the Split,* State University of New York Press, Albany, 1994

Netherton, Morris and Nancy Shiffrin, *Past Lives Therapy,* William Morrow, New York, 1978

Penrose, Roger, *The Emperor's New Mind,* Oxford University Press, New York, 1989

Persinger, M. A. and S. Krippner, "Dream ESP experiments and geomagnetic activity," The Journal of the American Society for Psychical Research, Vol. 83, 1989

Puthoff, Harold A, "Source of vacuum electromagnetic zero-point energy,"Physical Review A, 40.9, 1989

——, and Russell Targ, "A perceptual channel for information transfer over kilometer distances: historical perspective and recent research" Proceedings of the IEEE, Vol. 64, 1976

Ray, Paul H, "American Lives," Noetics Sciences Review, Spring 1996

Robert, Michel, *Le sol,* Masson, Paris, 1996

Rosenthal, R. "Combining results of independent studies," Psychological Bulletin, 85, 1978

Russell, Peter, *The Global Brain Awakens: Our New Evolutionary Leap,* Global Brain, Palo Alto, CA, 1995

Stevenson, Ian, *Children Who Remember Previous Lives,* University Press of Virginia, Charlottesville, 1987

Targ, Russell, and Harold A. Puthoff, "Information transmission under conditions of sensory shielding," in Nature, Vol 251, 1974

Targ, Russell and K. Harary, *The Mind Race,* Villard Books, New York, 1984

Tarnas, Richard, *The Passion of the Western Mind,* Ballantine Books, New York, 1993

Tart, Charles, *States of Consciousness,* Dutton, New York, 1975.

Tiller, William A. "Subtle energies in energy medicine", Frontier Perspectives, 4,2 , Spring 1995

Ullman, M. and S. Krippner, *Dream Studies and Telepathy: An Experimental Approach,* Parapsychology Foundation, New York, 1970

Varvoglis, Mario, "Goal-directed- and observer-dependent PK: An evaluation of the conformance-behavior model and the observation theories," The Journal of the American Society for Psychical Research, 80, 1986

Wagner, M.W. and M. Monnet, "Attitudes of college professors toward extrasensory perception," Zetetic Scholar, 5, 1979

Woolger, Roger, *Other Lives, Other Selves,* Doubleday, NY, 1987.

RECENT PUBLICATIONS BY THE AUTHOR

The Age of Bifurcation, The Key to Understanding the Changing World, Gordon & Breach, New York and London, 1991
Creative Evolution, ed, Gordon & Breach, New York, 1991
New Lectures on Systems Philosophy, Chinese Social Science Press, Beijing, 1992
The Evolution of Cognitive Maps, New Paradigms for the 21st Century, ed with I Masulli, Gordon & Breach, New York, 1992
The Creative Cosmos, Toward a Unified Science of Matter, Life and Mind, Floris Books, Edinburgh, 1993
A Multicultural Planet, Diversity and Dialogue in our Common Future, Oneworld, Oxford, 1993
Vision 2020, Restructuring Chaos for Global Order, Gordon & Breach, New York, 1994
The Choice: Evolution or Extinction; the Thinking Person's Guide to Global Problems, Tarcher/Putnam, Los Angeles, 1994
Wissenschaft und Wirklichkeit, Insel Verlag, Frankfurt, 1995
The Interconnected Universe, Conceptual Foundations of Transdisciplinary Unified Theory, World Scientific, Singapore and London, 1995
Frieden Durch Dialog, ed with Frank Shure, Aufbau, Berlin, 1995
Changing Visions, Human Cognitive Maps, Past, Present and Future, with Robert Artigiani, Alan Combs and Vilmos Csányi, Praeger, Westport; Adamantine Press, London 1996
The Systems View of the World, Hampton Press, New Jersey, 1996
Evolution: the General Theory, Hampton Press, New Jersey, 1996
The Whispering Pond, a Personal Guide to the Emerging Vision of Science, Element Books, Shaftesbury, UK, Rockport, MA, 1996
The Insight Edge, An Introduction to the Theory and Practice of Evolutionary Management, with Christopher Laszlo, Quorum Books, Westport, 1997
I Dialoghi: Ervin Laszlo, Di Renz Editore, Rome, 1997

INDEX

OTHER TITLES FROM GAIA BOOKS

ALSO IN THE GAIA CLASSICS SERIES

THIS LAND IS OUR LAND
Marion Shoard
ISBN 1 85675 064 7
£10.99

A fully updated reissue of Shoard's seminal work of 1987, to reflect growing concerns about rights of access to land, and the care of the countryside.

EARTH TO SPIRIT
David Pearson
ISBN 1 85675 046 9
£11.99

In the past, buildings expressed a harmony between people, land and cosmos that linked Earth to Spirit. David Pearson explores the new architecture that honours old traditions yet uplifts them with current ideas - from home and garden to community design.

THE GAIA ATLAS OF CITIES
Herbert Girardet
ISBN 1 85675 097 3
£11.99

Adopted by Habitat II, the UN Conference on Human Settlements and the Future of Cities. This book takes a new look at the creation of cities, exploring their design and ways to develop them as self-sustaining environments.

WEALTH BEYOND MEASURE
Paul Ekins
ISBN 1 85675 050 7
£11.99

How to create a sustainable and humane society. The book presents 'green' economics and illustrates how co-operation at a local level can really help create equality of health and wealth.

To request a full catalogue of titles published by Gaia Books please call 01453 752985, fax 01453 752987 or write to Gaia Books Ltd., 20 High Street, Stroud, Gloucestershire, GL5 1AS e-mail address gaiabook@star.co.uk Internet address http://www.gaiabooks.co.uk